THE SHOPS OF IRELAND

Leab

Dubli
Baile Át'

SEAN ROTHERY

THE SHOPS OF IRELAND

Drawings by the author

FRANCES LINCOLN LIMITED
PUBLISHERS

Frances Lincoln Limited
4 Torriano Mews
Torriano Avenue
London NW5 2RZ
www.franceslincoln.com

The Shops of Ireland
Text and illustrations copyright © Sean Rothery 2009, 1978
Images Courtesy of the National Library of Ireland
First Frances Lincoln edition 2009
First published in 1978 by Gill and Macmillan Ltd, Dublin

A catalogue record for this book is available from the British Library.

978-0-7112-3060-6

Printed and bound in China

1 2 3 4 5 6 7 8 9

For Nuala

Contents

A nineteenth-century shop in Derry

Acknowledgements

I wish to express my gratitude to Cement Roadstone Holdings Ltd for a grant which helped my research for this book.

The idea for the book was born when working with students of the Department of Architecture in Bolton Street College of Technology on a project for European Architectural Heritage Year, 1975. I am deeply indebted to Derry O'Connell, a former student, for his enthusiasm and dedication and for providing photographs and information on most of the Ulster shops in the book.

My grateful thanks also to Maura Fennell, librarian, for her unfailing enthusiasm and assistance and to her staff in the library of the Bolton Street College of Technology.

The following also helped or contributed in some way to the book. The Library, Trinity College, Dublin; the National Library; the National Gallery; An Taisce, the National Trust; the Ulster Architectural Heritage Society Lists. I acknowledge the help of the late Raymond McGrath, who supplied me with photographs and information on his early work. The following also gave information and helped to solve puzzles – Brendan McSharry, Eoghan Buckley, Neil Noonan, Edward Squire, J. B. Malone, Mrs J. Kiernan, C. E. B. Brett, T. F. McNamara, F. P. Stephens, Colm McKernan, Niall Montgomery, Edward McParland, Nora Relihan and Joseph Davis.

I acknowledge my debt to the scholarship of many writers in the field. The works I consulted are listed in the bibliography at the end of the book.

The most important contributors to the book were the owners of all the shops I have visited and illustrated – many of whom helped me with information.

Finally, eternal thanks to my wife Nuala for patiently reading and correcting my manuscript and for making sense where none existed.

Illustrations

I am grateful to the National Gallery of Ireland for permission for the reproduction of pictures and to the National Library for permission to reproduce the photographs from the Lawrence Collection. Birch's shop and Peter Jones' shop in London are drawn from old photographs in various books. Sangster's umbrella shop is from Nathaniel Whittock's book and Easiwork Kitchen Cabinets is from old photographs and information from Raymond McGrath. Most of the Ulster shops are from photographs and sketches by Derry O'Connell. All of the remaining illustrations are from my own photographs, notes or sketches.

The cover design is from a painting by Michael Lunt and is reproduced by kind permission of Roadstone Ltd.

Introduction

More than thirty years have passed since *The Shops of Ireland* was first published. Immense changes have occurred in those three decades, not the least being the transformation of an island on the periphery of the continent of Europe to a nation firmly embedded in the affairs of a growing European Union. The population of Ireland, North and South, having stagnated from the beginning of the twentieth century, has grown strongly, resulting in a vastly increased expansion of towns and cities. This development has led, inevitably, to a further erosion of the vernacular tradition of small-scale shop design.

It was still possible in the early 1970s, when much of the exploration for this work was done, to see in many a town or village a little shop that was unchanged, in function or appearance, for at least a hundred years. Even in the cities, a few specimens of the unbroken tradition of vernacular shop design lived on. Now, of those illustrated, Price's Medical Hall on Dublin's Clare Street is the sole unchanged survivor in the capital, six have vanished and all the remaining examples are either altered in appearance or function, while a few are shuttered, perhaps awaiting oblivion. Outside the cities, in towns and villages, the tradition of the carefully crafted shop front continued to decline and now may be just a memory.

The arrival of the huge new shopping centres, often at the edge of towns, combined with the spectacular rise of car dependency, seemed to hasten the death of the main street small shop. Salvation, in the form of marketing chains, helped to keep the old street alive, but the charm of individuality was lost in the birth of the 'mini market': the butcher, the baker, the chemist, the newsagent, the hardware merchant were marshalled into neat aisles and electronic outlets replaced the old wooden counters. The worst effect of the grouping into chain stores was the imposition of new plastic fascias, often crude and insensitive, over the original hand-painted or crafted wood name boards: the 'corporate' image was paramount.

One major change in the Irish landscape of the early twenty-first century may yet herald a lifeline for traditional urban architecture. New motorways and dual-carriageways now bypass places where main streets became arterial routes choked with day-long traffic. There are opportunities now to restore a sense of place to these main streets, and village cores and local communities can reclaim ownership of their inheritance.

The survival of the traditional Irish shop front, at least as a memory of a past rich heritage of folk art, may at last be recognized as a desirable objective. The single biggest stimulus to this is the enormous success of the Tidy Towns Competition, which began on a small scale in 1958 and has now grown into a countryside enterprise, with more than 700 entries. In addition to the main awards for best towns and best villages, there are a large number of special awards and one of these is for shop fronts. This category is described as an award for 'The best maintained traditional shop front or the best designed modern shop front.'

A more recent and equally important initiative is the setting up of the National Inventory of Architectural Heritage. County Surveys have been published for most of the Republic of Ireland, with work on the remaining counties proceeding. The Ulster Architectural Heritage Society continues to support the conservation of the historic architecture of Northern Ireland. The inclusion of surviving traditional shop fronts is a valuable component of the various inventories. Many more original specimens may still exist, at least partly intact, but buried behind modern plastic and plywood cladding. The removal of this cheap veneer may reveal long-forgotten gems that are easy to restore. The listing in these surveys of traditional buildings, crafted shop fronts, hand painted name boards and plaster-decorated façades may halt or slow the destruction of a lively folk architecture that contributes immeasurably to the Irish townscape.

Dublin, January 2009

South Main Street, Wexford, c.1900

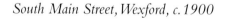

History

Early History

Shops were originally the workplaces of tradesmen and craftsmen. The goods were made in the workshop and sold directly to customers who came to inspect the finished articles or to have their own special orders made up. Shops selling foods of various kinds developed directly from the stalls set up by farmers in market towns to sell their surplus produce.

An entry in the CALENDAR OF ANCIENT RECORDS OF DUBLIN for 1651 gives an interesting picture of the variety and type of tradesmen and craftworkers who had workshops in the city. The list of applicants for admission to franchise includes a cutler, smith, goldsmith, clockmaker, saddlers, glovers, tailors, tallow chandlers, shoemaker, slater, butchers, shermen, trunk maker, farrier, mason, baker, brazier and joiner. They were admitted 'By special grace and on fine of . . . a paire of gloves to Mistris Maioresse' and 'one butt of sack delivered to Mr. Maior free of all chardges'.

Friction between shopkeepers and street hawkers and regraters (dealers) appeared to have been common. The CALENDAR OF ANCIENT RECORDS for the year 1656 recorded a complaint from the freemen of the city about the *constant and continuall intrusions of severall persons of severall nations, who daily buy and sell by grosse and retayle as well out of marketts as in marketts, open shops and private houses – without any regard of the customs and priviledges of the said cittie.*

In 1661 the CALENDAR gives some evidence of the goods sold by the street hawkers and traders and the competition they provided to the legitimate freemen shopkeepers of the ancient city of Dublin. The freemen presented a petition to the Assembly: *Sheweinge there are a very greate number of loose, idle and disordered persons without difference of age or sexe, that give themselves over to sloath and idleness, sittinge in most places of this cittie and suburbs, and, sometimes goeinge about the cittie with aples, nutts and about other idle imployments, as alsoe certaine of such persons that sell sneesinge salte and tobacco, which tends much to the impoverishing of the freemen shopkeepers that doe trade in such commodities.*

Rather drastic remedies were proposed by the legitimate business interests of the city of Dublin to deal with this unfair competition. In 1659 there was a petition for the: *Suppressinge of the greate number of idle women, and maydens that sitt in most streetes of this cittie, sellinge of aples, orenges, lemons and other regrateinge of egges, henns, and severall other commodities, to the grate prejudice of the inhabitants of this cittie: and also for the suppressinge of the many idle boyes that are in the said cittie and have noe lawful callinge or way of livelyhoode.* It was to be ordered *that*

forthwith there shall bee a lardge cage sett in the Cornemarkett, where the beadles and constables are to imprison all beggars, idle women, and maids sellinge aples and orenges and all regraters, and all idle boys.

The earliest shops were open fronted, having a counter between the shop and the street and shops like these existed in second century Rome. Later developments of larger shops, possibly workshops having apprentices and craftsmen employed by a master, allowed open access to the shop along the front and put the counter on one side at right angles to the street. This plan form still exists today.

The open fronted shop as a general type lasted well into the eighteenth century. Contemporary engravings of London show open fronted shops beside glazed examples. A Malton print of 1793 in the National Gallery in Dublin shows open fronted butchers' shops under Dutch gabled houses beside St Patrick's Cathedral.

The open front in fact existed until the 1950s for a few specialist food shops, particularly butchers', poulterers' and fish shops. The reason for this could have been that all of these products were rather pungent and the circulation of fresh air allowed the smell to be bearable or actually palatable. Food hygiene laws and the invention of freezers have put an end to this chapter in the history of shops, which has lasted at least since Imperial Rome.

The open fronted shop of mediaeval times, itself hardly changed at all from the shops of the Roman Forum of Trajan, was closed at night by wooden shutters. These were usually divided in two, the lower section forming an extension to the counter and the upper section hinged outwards to form a protection for the goods on display outside.

The names of streets and laneways, many surviving, in mediaeval cities give a clue to the type of trade carried on in these places many years ago. In the old city of York there is a Tanner's Row, a Swinegate and the Shambles. The Castle Museum in York has a reconstructed street of old shops from the city, each with window displays and interior of the period. The Shambles in York was the street of open fronted butchers' shops and a reconstruction of the street in mediaeval times would be horrific to our modern eyes. The narrow street with the upper parts of the houses overhanging and almost touching each other, shutting out the light and air, was a Dante's inferno. Shouting shopowners and crowds of customers inspecting the bloody carcasses laid out on the wooden counters or hanging from rails along the shop front constituted the scene, while an open channel in the middle of the cobbled street carried away water and offal waste.

In Dublin's mediaeval city the names again give a picture of the life in the streets in those days. Skinner's Row beside Christchurch probably provided the leather for the shoemakers in Shoemaker's Lane nearby. Fishamble Street was the early fishmongers' equivalent of the butchers' shambles. Although the line of the street still exists, none of the earliest buildings survive. Winetavern Street is a romantic survival of a trade from the sailing ships which tied up at Wood Quay.

The CALENDAR OF ANCIENT RECORDS OF DUBLIN mentions that there were 1500 'innes and alehouses' in the city in 1667 when, according to Maurice Craig, the population was about 30,000, growing to 58,000 in 1681. The CALENDAR in 1652 announced that the

Corporation of Butchers wished to have a lease of a room 'over the Fleshambles of the cittie in Cornemarkett'.

Glazing of shop fronts only began towards the end of the seventeenth century and the earliest evidence of this appears to be from Holland. In London and Paris the beginning of the eighteenth century saw the rapid spread of glazed shop fronts in all the principal shopping streets. Addison in the TATLER wrote, somewhat sarcastically: *Having lately observed several warehouses, nay, private shops, that stand upon Corinthian pillars, and whole rows of tin pots showing themselves, in order to their sale, through a sash window.*

Birch's confectioner's shop was typical of the mid eighteenth century and once stood in Cornhill, London. Dan's ENGLISH SHOP FRONTS (1907) called this the oldest shop front still existing in the City of London. It was removed in 1926 to the Victoria and Albert Museum.

The round headed windows and small glazed units were to remain a characteristic of shops for many years. The spandrils with delicate wood carving are in the elegant style of Robert Adam (1728–92) but Dan considered that this shop was earlier than Adam, who only settled in London after his Grand Tour in 1758.

John Summerson in GEORGIAN LONDON stated that it was doubtful if any shop existed in London which could clearly be dated earlier than the mid eighteenth century, but that many later eighteenth-century shops existed in London minus the original Georgian glazing bars.

Shop, Corn Hill, London

Another typical mid eighteenth-century shop design was the symmetrical front with a door in the middle of two convex windows.

Shop, Norton Folgate, London

Peter Jones, Son and Mundy was in Norton Folgate, London and its design was probably the most commonplace of the eighteenth century.

This was the type of shop which was certainly very common in eighteenth-century Dublin, then an important city in relation to London. The population of Dublin in 1750, according to Maurice Craig, was 130,000 and between one fifth and one sixth the size of London and had 'no rivals in the three Kingdoms'.

Malton Prints in the National Gallery, Dublin, show many examples of standard design and elegant curved-front shops. These are usually in the background to views of large public buildings. One of the most interesting of these prints, dated 1792, shows simple shops with small window panes beside the Tholsel. A print of 1797 of Thomas Street shows a surprisingly neat and regular row of shops.

Shops in Castle Street, Cork, in an engraving of 1796 reproduced in LIFE IN IRELAND by L. M. Cullen, show round headed windows, fanlights over doors and regular fascias with names.

Sadly none of these beautiful 18th century shops remain in Dublin, although a few slightly curved windows still exist in shops throughout the country.

Early shops had no numbers and were often identified by elaborate signs as well as the name of the owner. In mid-seventeenth-century Dublin the CALENDAR OF ANCIENT RECORDS mentions the 'Signe of the Wandering Jew' a house near St Werburgh's and the

Malton's View of the Tholsel, Dublin, with eighteenth-century shops (1792) Courtesy of the National Gallery of Ireland

'Bear and Ragged Staff' on the south side of Castle Street. Later references include the 'Pestle and Mortar' on Skinners Row and the 'Three Wolves Heads' on High Street. Towards the end of the eighteenth century the influence of the books of craftsmen-architects began to be felt. One of these was William Pain who in 1763 produced THE BUILDER'S POCKET TREASURE, ETC. Other craftsmen-architects included J. Crunden and A. Swan who were themselves carpenters and they wrote for the benefit of other carpenters and craftsmen. All the writers of these design books emphasised the importance of a good knowledge of the Classical Orders of Architecture. These books, like the famous THE CITY AND COUNTRY BUILDER'S AND WORKMAN'S TREASURY OF DESIGNS (1750) by Batty Langley became the source books of the ordinary craftsman and builder of town and country.

The NEW PRACTICAL BUILDER AND WORKMAN'S COMPANION (1823) by Peter Nicholson had some beautiful engravings of shop designs which were probably very influential in shop design in later years.

The drawing from Taylor's book shows the beginning of elements of shop front design which were to establish themselves for over a century to come. The display windows were framed and emphasised with classical columns. The doorway was given a decorative fanlight but not over-emphasised to take away from the windows and the classical entablature was found to be ideal for finishing off the top of the design and providing a place for the name of the shop.

Shop, Strabane, Co. Tyrone
This shop is one of the oldest in the country. The whole front is slightly curved and the windows are framed by simply capped slender columns. This was a later development of the mid eighteenth-century double bow window shop. Pilasters replaced the doorposts and fanlights were introduced over the entrance doors.

From Taylor, DESIGNS FOR SHOP FRONTS *(1792).*

Roger Hart in ENGLISH LIFE IN THE 18TH CENTURY (1970) stated that the shops of eighteenth-century London were the most famous in Europe. He quotes Dr Johnson's suggestion to Goldsmith: 'Let us take a walk from Charing Cross to Whitechapel through I suppose the greatest series of shops in the world.' C. P. Moritz, a German visitor to London in 1782 notes: *Especially in the Strand, where one shop jostles another and people of different trades often live in the same house, it is surprising to see how from bottom to top the various houses often display large signboards with painted letters. Everyone who lives and works in the same house sports his signboard over the door; indeed there is not a cobbler whose name and trade is not to be read in large golden characters . . . I have found dealer in Spirituous Liquors to be the most frequent inscription among them. In London care is taken to show . . . all works of art and industry to the public . . . Such a street often resembles a well organized show cabinet.*

Into the Nineteenth Century

Towards the mid nineteenth century the competition from shop owners for attention and advertisement of each establishment led to an explosion of different designs for shop fronts and a breakaway from the standard and serene uniformity of the earlier Georgian period. Specialist books on shop front design now appeared. The most influential of these was probably Nathaniel Whittock who in 1840 produced ON THE CONSTRUCTION AND DECORATION OF THE SHOP FRONTS OF LONDON. Other source books of the time were T. King's SHOP FRONTS (1830), an advocate of Moorish and Egyptian design, and J. Young DESIGNS FOR SHOP FRONTS (1830).

The lovely old shop front in Smithfield is one of the oldest surviving fronts in Dublin. The illustration is a possible reconstruction of the original front, as today the left hand larger round headed window has an extra door rather crudely set into the space. J. B. Malone has researched the history of the house and he considers that the front can be dated to about the 1830s. The original owners were the Carolan family who had a connection with the licensed trade in the area for over 100 years. In 1909 the shop was a grocer and wine merchant's.

Shop, High Street, Ballymena, Co. Antrim
The description given in the survey list
ANTRIM AND BALLYMENA *by the Ulster Architectural Heritage Society aptly sums up this lovely building and urgent steps must be taken to restore and preserve it: 'A first rate Georgian block, five bays by three storeys, with an exceptionally fine classical shop front along its entire length; built of basalt with brick trim and Georgian glazed windows above the ground floor. The shop front has a long entablature supported on five fluted Ionic columns that are finely carved. They are irregularly spaced and between each column is a tripartite Georgian window, an extremely elegant late eighteenth-century door in a curved segmental recess, then the main shop front, a central door with curved glazed windows on either side, and finally a coach entrance to the yard behind. This shop front must be one of the best remaining of its period anywhere in Ireland and ought to be preserved.'*

Old Shop, Smithfield, Dublin

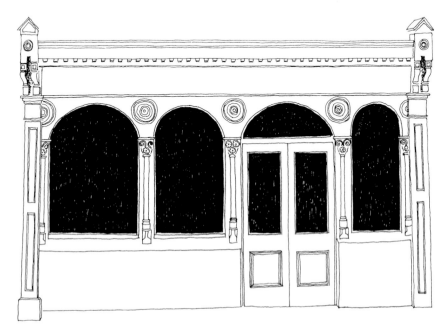

Old shop front, Youghal, Co. Cork
This beautiful shop front is lovingly
restored and painted although the
building is no longer used as a shop.
The design is strikingly similar to
designs in the source books of the 1830s
and 1840s. The continuation of the
pilasters forming separate little end
pieces to the name fascia is particularly
refined and unusual.

The design, now much mutilated by many layers of paint, has an air of early Georgian about it with the almost semi-circular window heads and decorated wood spandrils. The colonettes are decorated with rosettes and volutes. Restored and with the layers of paint stripped away, it could be a beautiful link with the past history of this part of Dublin.

A letter from 'octogenarian' in the IRISH BUILDER of 15 February 1898, gives a fascinating description of Dublin shops of the 1840s. He described the many old print shops north and south of the Liffey, including Le Pettits in Henry Street and McCleery's in Nassau Street: *There was Wisehearts' old shop in Suffolk Street where the well-to-do purchased prints and pictures and the apprentice boys and workmen looked out for the last number of Wiseheart's VOCALIST, SENTIMENTAL OR HUMOROUS SONGSTER containing the newest songs sung in the city taverns. Nolan's 'Noah's Ark' had ornithological specimens and its monkeys as well as the newest toys. Coynes in Capel Street had 'attractions for Catholics – in books and prints' and Richard Coyne in his black suit, frilled shirt, knee breeches and silver buckled shoes was a pleasant sight. Richard Glennon, the naturalist in Suffolk Street had an attractive window for antiquaries and juveniles; and 'he was not only a good bird-stuffer but a practical minded and intelligent man'. . . . Old Anglesea Street was attractive though its scores of bookshops [are] now nearly all dissipated . . . Dame Street and Parliament Street were strong in prints, music and musical instruments.*

The Regency period of design in the early part of the nineteenth century saw the appearance, according to John Summerson, of the designed shopping street and he mentions that the best example in London was Woburn Walk of 1822.

Edward McParland, however, in the 'The Wide Streets Commissioners: their importance for Dublin Architecture in the late 18th and early 19th century', IRISH GEORGIAN SOCIETY BULLETIN (1972), shows that shopping streets were being designed and executed in Dublin from 1799 onwards, a period when nothing similar was being attempted in England.

Summerson in GEORGIAN LONDON states: *Up to the Napoleonic period a shop front was never considered either as part of the facade of which it formed the base or as part of a consistent architectural panorama at street level. The designed shopping street belongs to the Regency and after, and even then such streets were modest affairs, often mere passages, situated at the edge of big shopping districts.*

The grand scale of the proposed elevations of Westmoreland Street and D'Olier Street by Henry A. Baker and the elevation to Sackville Street by Thomas Sherrard now in the Public Record Office, Dublin, is most impressive and certainly if the streets existed in their entirety today they would have a profound effect on the townscape of central Dublin.

Developments in Paris around this time included the great colonnade of shops along the Rue de Rivoli, a rather dull and repetitive design and a nondescript background to the immense Jardin des Tuileries. The Dublin designs would possibly have had

Malton's view from Capel Street, Dublin, towards the Royal Exchange (1797) Courtesy of the National Gallery of Ireland

more character. The most architecturally interesting scheme in Paris was the Cour Batave of 1791 by architects Sobre and Happe, which was a large block with a central courtyard, and the shop elevations show large windows alternating with entrance doors.

Edward McParland sums up the work and importance of the Wide Street Commissioners: *Modern Dublin between the canals is largely as planned by them. Their planning of Dublin differed from the planning of other Irish Towns and cities (although Cork had its own Wide Streets Commissioners) in that they rationalized an existing plan instead of laying out geometrical abstractions in previously undeveloped suburbs. It differed too in being a corporate effort on the part of politically powerful men, who, it has been suggested, were to some degree politically motivated in what they did. Their political power however, had to be fused with cultural enlightenment and that this happened is abundantly clear in the personalities of the pre-Union Commissioners. They were quite clear that their model was London and its contemporary developments: they were experienced enough to see that London alone did not provide the answer to all of their building needs and so, in borrowing from Continental examples, they revived, in concept if not in execution, the Roman Renaissance type of palace facade with ground floor shops. Baker's executed elevations in Westmoreland Street predate similar developments in England by about 15 years.*

Controversy became common about shop design in the early part of the nineteenth century when designs began to break away from the discipline and serenity of the Georgian period. Georgian shops in Dublin, certainly as portrayed by Malton, appeared to be related to the typically Irish Georgian proportions with adroitness and elegance. The small paned windows dividing up the otherwise considerably out of scale large shop window, had a major influence on the harmony of the streetscape.

A critic in THE BUILDER of 1848 complained that the classical orders were unsuitable for shops because the openings which had to be left between the columns for the display windows were too large for classical proportions and asked 'why should a style be employed merely for the purpose of being mangled?'. The large windows were reasonably acceptable when divided by glazing bars in classical small scale proportions, but the arrival of plate glass changed everything.

Sangster's umbrella shop in London was built in the magnificent Louis XIV style and triumphantly heralded the possibilities of plate glass. The ARCHITECTURAL MAGAZINE in 1838 describes the Louis Quatorze style as *one of the latest improvements in this department; and in combination with the immense panes of plate glass now used, and accompanied by rich gilding on a pure white ground, it has a striking and most magnificent appearance.* Mary Eldridge wrote a very valuable and detailed article for the March 1958 ARCHITECTURAL REVIEW on the plate glass shop front. She stated that the removal of the excise duty on glass in 1845 removed a serious constraint on the use of plate glass in shop windows.

Raymond McGrath in GLASS IN ARCHITECTURE noted that plate glass used in shop fronts met with a mixed reception in the nineteenth century. A correspondent to THE BUILDER of 18 September 1852 said: *The improvement that has been observable during the last few years in the appearance of the commercial and other buildings lining the principal streets of our metropolis, and also in the larger towns throughout the Kingdom, may*

Hardware shop, Castlecomer, Co. Kilkenny

Chemist's shop, Castlecomer, Co. Kilkenny

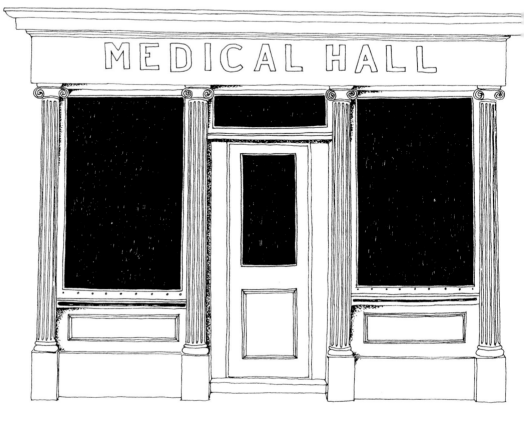

be attributed mainly to one cause – the use of plate glass. *Those who look back some ten or twenty years and remember the long rows of meaningless (and, in many instances, lop sided cant bowed) windows, with a very large proportion of the light-room blinded by gratings of sash-bars, and the glass itself very attentuated, and having a blotchy and uneven appearance; and when the fascia board was scooped out at the ends to give the desired return projection to the incongruous cornice above – will look with surprise at the costly arrangements which now take their place.* However, he then goes on to say: *There is yet much to be done in this path. We have in many instances yet to see the upper stories of shopped houses carried by something substantial, and not having the appearance of being supported on glass!*

The writer is rather sour about the eighteenth-century shopping streets, but no doubt to the mid nineteenth-century interested person, the technology of plate glass heralded a new order and was as progressive as the Westminster Act of 1762 which made improvements to the streets. One of these was that large signs had to be fixed flat against the wall instead of sticking out and allowing rainwater to drip on the passer-by.

There was no doubt about the attitude of the DUBLIN BUILDER to progress at the time. An article in the issue of 1 June 1859 rejoiced that: *Old Dublin was gradually consigning to oblivion her quaintness, her peculiarities and, we may add, her deformities – ill fashioned shop-fronts with squat storey-posts, many squared sashes, entablatures mean or tawdrily decorated, pigeon-hole windows above, and dangerous gratings – receptacles for dust etc. – below, are being replaced by lofty plate glass, consoled and richly entablatured elevations transmitting light to basement through handsome cast-iron work in the pedestals and suitably decorated in all their parts.*

These delightful little shops, obviously by the same craftsman designer, are in Castlecomer, Co. Kilkenny and are a typical design from the mid-nineteenth century. Here is the established architectural grammar of the period; classical columns, in these examples a diminutive but perfectly scaled Ionic, and a neat classical entablature for the name panel.

John Rohan's shop is in Youghal, Co. Cork and is a delightful example of the daring and elegant use of the larger glass sizes which became available in the mid-nineteenth century. The lettering is pure Art Nouveau and belongs to the end of the century.

Main Street,
Wexford, c.1900

The Village Shop

Old Shop, Askeaton, Co. Limerick
This tiny shop probably dates from the end of the eighteenth century. It has not been used as a shop in living memory, but like many former house shops in Ireland, it still retains its shop window. This has been made larger than the house window and colonettes with foliated caps denote the commercial function.

The shops of the small towns and villages were much more modest than the shops of the cities. These country shops served the needs of the farming community in the surrounding rural area whose needs were also modest, a combination of poverty and self-sufficiency.

The shops were generally those of the village craftsmen – the carpenters, blacksmiths, wheelwrights, saddlers and millers who served the functional needs of the farmers. The earliest shops of small villages would simply have been set up in the ground floor of the house and have used the house window for display.

House shops, with thatched roofs in many cases, similar to the shop illustrated, in Kildorrery, were the kind of shops which existed in towns and villages of Ireland right through into the twentieth century.

The little shop in Newcastle West is typical of the workshops of village craftsmen which were common throughout Ireland.

Pamela Horn in LABOURING LIFE IN THE VICTORIAN COUNTRYSIDE quotes a contemporary description of the interior of a shoemaker's shop in Victorian England: *His wall and ceiling were hung with wooden lasts on which the boots and shoes were made; his bench had little slots for nails, sprigs and wooden pegs. The shoemaker sat with his bootjack between his knees, his mouth full of brass sprigs which he spat out as required, and he knocked them into the heels and soles of the boots with the back of an old worn-down rasp.*

A craftsman like the saddler and harness maker was a great necessity in a farming area. He made all the harness used for the different tasks of farming. Different equipment was needed for ploughing, carting and other farm tasks and each owner had a special interest in the harness he required for each animal. The saddler was as well known as the village spademaker, who enjoyed the reputation once held by the swordmaker and like him survived by his skill and craft.

Shoemaker's Shop, Newcastle West, Co. Limerick
This tradesman's house in Newcastle West – once thatched – housed a shoemaker. The larger window was more for the provision of light to a workbench, than for the display of goods.

Old Shop, Kildorrery, Co. Cork
This old shop is, sadly, in ruinous condition in the lovely village of Kildorrery. The actual shop front with its simple fascia and tiny wood pilasters is quite developed. The door and window without any trimmings sufficed in many places right into the twentieth century. Everybody knew the shop keeper and the goods stocked and therefore design trimmings were considered unnecessary and possibly pretentious.

Thatched Pub-Shop, Kingscourt, Co. Cavan
Cartlan's lovely old pub shop is in the main street of Kingscourt. The building is probably eighteenth century although the sash windows and shop front are certainly nineteenth century additions.

Cartlans again illustrates the multifariousness of the business carried on in many of the general stores of country areas. Grocery, provisions and hardware often went side by side with the business of a pub, thus satisfying the several needs of a customer from rural parts in one shop.

Another characteristic of country stores is evident in Cartlans. This was the practice of obscuring the lower parts of the window to provide privacy for the customers of the bar from prying eyes in the street. Display windows were considered unnecessary. The archway to the yard behind is again a characteristic device of Irish towns. This allowed access to the rear without disturbing the rhythm of the street architecture.

Pamela Horn in her study LABOURING LIFE IN THE VICTORIAN COUNTRYSIDE quotes from the minute books of a co-operative society in England to give a picture of the sort of goods in demand at the time. These goods included: *105 sacks of flour, nine firkins of butter, eight sides of bacon, a chest of green tea, coffee, sugar treacle, pepper, ground ginger, bacon pigs, beef, pork, lamb, five cwt. of soap, ipecacuana wine (used as a purgative), six dozen broom heads, 3 dozen zinc buckets, nails, slippers, soda, notepaper and envelopes, snuff, tobacco, cough drops, blacking, flax and hemp for the shoemakers, paper bags and ten gallons of hair oil.*

The photographs of the Lawrence collection show advertisements for many of the above goods on shop windows or signs, and in many views the quantity of brooms and buckets hanging on outside display is remarkable; an indication, no doubt, of the necessity for continual sweeping of dusty floors. The photographs themselves give a graphic indication of the state of the streets!

Larger houses with shops on the ground floor similar to Wrens of Castleisland once stood in towns in every part of Ireland. The architecture of Wrens is in the late Georgian tradition which lasted in Ireland until the end of the nineteenth century. The three stories is characteristic of the larger villages and towns and instead of the parapet (common in the cities) the gutter is supported on stone, concrete or wood brackets. The house is articulated grandly from its neighbours by strongly expressed quoins and the important windows have projecting weathered hoods. The shopfront is graceful and delightful with the interesting device of carrying the motif of the round headed window across the fanlight. Originally the shop windows would have had a sash bar horizontally across the centre to give an economic glass pane size. The spandrils between the rounded headed windows are glazed, characteristically, in trefoil form. This gives a more delicate effect than the alternative method, also common, of filling the spandrils with a carved wood design.

The large two storey thatched house is a feature of vernacular building along the eastern part of Ireland notably in Co. Wexford, Co. Down, Co. Meath and north Co. Dublin. Some of the houses have been dated to the late seventeenth century. The tradition, notable in Cartlans of Kingscourt, of articulating the individual building in the street is carried out by painting the quoins and the flat plastered doorcase black.

Shop and House, Castleisland, Co. Kerry
This old shop and house is a typical mid-nineteenth-century example of the small town architecture of the period. The style is robust and unpretentious. The upper windows have, unfortunately, been replaced with modern standard casement windows, which spoil the facade. The drawing shows a probable elevation of the original windows.

Bridge Street and Main Street,
Skibbereen, Co. Cork, c. 1900

The Late Nineteenth Century

Shaw's NEW CITY PICTORIAL DIRECTORY (1850) is an interesting publication, since it shows elevations of the principal streets of Dublin. The drawings are rather rudimentary but the designs shown are likely to be reasonably accurate. Old bow fronted shops are shown on the quays near St Paul's Church and the traders' names are also given. The book has several advertisements including one with an engraving of the shop front of John Dillon, 46 High Street. This was a single bow-fronted shop with the advertisement: 'Soap boiler, Tallow chandler and chemical mould candle manufacturer.'

J. Grant's shop in Kevin Street, closed for some time and recently boarded up prior to demolition, is rather interesting. The design is a direct link with the mediaeval open shop and shows simple and practical developments. The open front has been replaced with an upward opening sash window which allowed a projecting tray of goods to be on display. Shops like this still exist in Irish towns and nineteenth-century photographs show that this type of shop was the most common one found in the poorer parts of the cities.

There was a marked contrast in the late nineteenth-century city between the prosperous middle class areas and the older densely populated and poorest areas.

Old shop, Kevin Street, Dublin

Friedrich Engels in THE CONDITION OF THE WORKING CLASS IN ENGLAND IN 1844 gives an interesting comment on the shops of the Victorian city and a plausible theory of the forces which gave the city its form.

In his account of Manchester he showed that the comfortable citizen travelling through that city need never know how the working class lived or need never be disturbed by the squalor and misery of the areas behind the main routes: *This is because the main streets which run from the Exchange in all directions out of the city are occupied almost uninterruptedly on both sides by shops, which are kept by members of the middle and lower middle classes. In their own interests these shopkeepers should keep up their shops in an outward appearance of cleanliness and respectability; and in fact they do so. To be sure these shops have nonetheless a concordant relation with those regions that lay stretched out behind them. Those shops which are situated in the commercial quarter or in the vicinity of the middle class residential districts are more elegant than those that serve to cover up (or as a facade for) the workers grimy cottages. Nevertheless even these latter adequately serve the purpose of hiding from the eyes of wealthy gentlemen and ladies with strong stomachs and weak nerves the misery and squalor that form the completing counterpart, the indivisible complement, of their riches and luxury.*

In Dublin, Clanbrassil Street and Charlemont Street still show the remains of modest but once neat shops which were backed by slum areas in the nineteenth and early twentieth centuries.

Combridges bookshop in Grafton Street, Dublin would certainly be one of the type of elegant shops mentioned by Engels. The large sheets of plate glass were available from about 1850, but this shop belongs in design and detail to the later part of the century. The name fascia is a splendid example of the type of expert work of shop

Bookshop, Grafton Street, Dublin This shop front dates from the late nineteenth century but an earlier bookshop existed at No. 18, Grafton Street. This was 'Cornish' which had an overhead sign 'Cheap book establishment' and it is illustrated in Shaw's NEW CITY PICTORIAL DIRECTORY (1850).

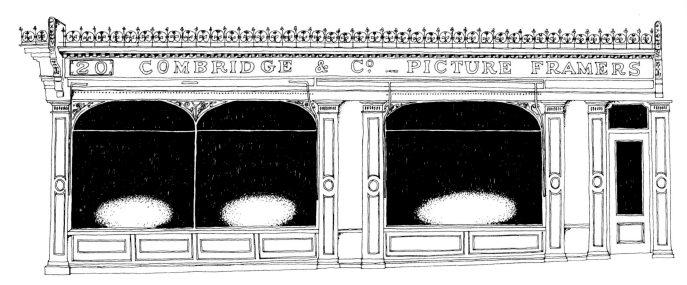

Art Shop, Grafton Street & Duke Street, Dublin
This shop front dates from about 1900. The original shop had a corner column. Shaw's Directory shows the earlier shop which was Hedgelong's and was a 'Theological & Miscellaneous Cheap Bookshop'.

fitting firms of the period. The letters are cut into a wood background and the fascia is then painted. Black was usual although green and red were also used for backgrounds. The letters themselves were picked out in gold leaf and the entire fascia was covered with large sheets of thick plate glass. The sloping stall boards were worked in the same manner and in Combridges the upper parts of the windows were painted black with gold lettering to match the larger sign. The original windows of Combridges as shown in early photographs of Grafton Street had typical white composition letters fixed to the upper parts of the windows. 'Lowest Prices for Cash Discount Booksellers'.

The Combridge shop which occupies the corner of Grafton Street and Duke Street is one of the most beautiful shops in Dublin. It was built at a later date than the bookshop. The present shop was built to match the bookshop on the Grafton Street front with a different but entirely appropriate elevation to Duke Street. The gracefully arched windows with delicate sash bars and carved wood spandrils form a splendid landmark in the street. The woodwork is painted entirely black and with the lettering in gold the shops are spectacular and exceptional and deserve to be cherished and preserved.

James Joyce in ULYSSES, describing the various perambulations through early twentieth-century Dublin, mentions many of the contemporary shops. Sadly, the two Combridges are probably the only unchanged shops remaining, which were landmarks for the city in a literary as well as a townscape sense: *Grafton Street gay with housed awnings lured his senses. Muslin prints, silk, dames and dowagers, jingle of harnesses, hoofthuds lowringing in the baking causeway. . . . He passed, dallying, the windows of Brown Thomas, silk mercers. Cascades of ribbons. Flimsy China silks. A tilted urn poured from its mouth a flood of bloodhued poplin; lustrous blood. The huguenots brought that here . . . Duke Street. Here we are. Must eat, The Burton. Feel better then. He turned Combridge's corner, still pursued.*

The Art Nouveau movement of design was a short but significant period from the 1890s into the first years of the twentieth century.

The most exuberant manifestations of the movement were in Belgium with the works of Victor Horta and Van de Velde, in Paris with Hector Guimard and in Barcelona with Antoni Gaudi. In Britain the work of Charles Rennie Mackintosh was to be the most significant of the period.

Art Nouveau had many and subtle influences on the design of shops both in the interiors and on the design of the fronts. The nervous and ungeometrical curves with, on the one hand, their affinity to the dynamic shapes of bones, and on the other, their reminiscences of plant forms, fascinated designers of the period who tried out these curves on the design of doorways, windows and particularly lettering.

CAFE AMERICAIN

In Paris the Cafe Americain designed by A. Moulins about 1900 showed many of the details which designers were to tentatively incorporate in shop design in Ireland in the early twentieth century. The plate glass is etched with flowery designs, the doors and window woodwork has subtle and ungeometrical curves and the lettering with its free flowing but robust shapes is similar to many Irish examples of the same period, notably John Rohan's shop in Youghal and P. A. Crane's photographer's shop in Enniscorthy, Co. Wexford.

P. A. CRANE

Photography shop, Enniscorthy, Co. Wexford

43

Another interesting shop design of the time in Paris was G. Fouquet's Jewellery Shop in Rue Royale. This shop was designed by the famous Art Nouveau designer Alphonse Mucha with exotic sculpture by Auguste Seysse.

Although Britain and Ireland did not join in with the exhuberance of Art Nouveau ornamentation in its wildest forms, there are many examples of the influence of the movement in little details of shop design, the search for which can be intriguing for the close observer. As well as in the lettering of the period, Art Nouveau influences can be seen particularly in chemists' shops with the details of doorway woodwork and etched designs on the glass. The plasterwork of Pat

Music Shop, Wellington Place, Belfast
Crymble's Music Shop in Wellington Place, Central Belfast, was designed by W. J. W. Roome and dates from 1903. The shop front shows many of the influences of Art Nouveau and the search at the turn of the century for novelty and richness in decoration. In particular the indulgence in high quality materials was typical of the time. In this design the most striking feature is the elaborate metal fascia with flowery embossed patterns and the large central plaque with the design of musical instruments on polished copper. There are flowery patterns interlaced with musical instruments in coloured mosaic on the spandrils over the large first floor arched window and the whole design is triumphantly signposted with the twin obelisks.

McAuliffe in the south west of the country shows many Art Nouveau mannerisms and the arts and crafts cum Art Nouveau influences on ceramic tile design can be seen in the very few surviving examples of tiled shops throughout the country.

The IRISH BUILDER of 1904 quotes a 'remarkable denunciation of L'Art Nouveau' delivered by one John Belcher A.R.A.: *An art forsooth, a pernicious trick easily acquired and applied alike to buildings or jewellery, furniture or dress, no matter what the nature of the material . . . all alike twisted to curves representing the final stages of vegetable decay and animal decrepitude, in defiance of all true principles of construction and beauty.*

Large scale re-development of areas levelled by slum clearance became a feature of the late nineteenth century. Some of this work was carried out by speculators who contributed some excellent blocks of houses with standard shops at street level. Dublin has many terraces of neat late Victorian houses with standard shopfronts embellished with simply decorated fascias and pilasters. Re-housing the working class and needy in new blocks which were sanitary and airy and provided many facilities like bathhouses, laundries and shops became desirable enterprises for the wealthy philanthropist towards the end of the nineteenth century.

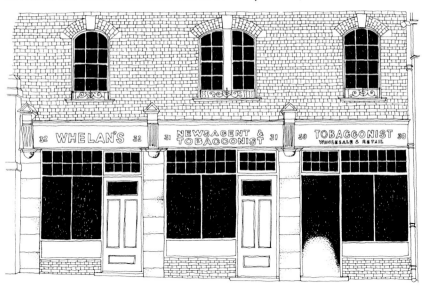

Shops, Iveagh buildings, Dublin

The Iveagh Buildings near St Patrick's Cathedral, Dublin were built by Lord Iveagh in 1901–1905 and provided flats, shops, a hostel and swimming baths. The architect was Joseph Smithem of London and Kaye Parry of Dublin was the supervising architect. The great bricklayers lock-out of 1905, which lasted for many months, considerably delayed this building and many others in Dublin at the time.

The shops although standardised and in dull colours with uniform lettering, are expertly detailed and neatly considered in relation to the windows of the flats overhead. There are several Art Nouveau influences in these buildings from the obviously Charles Rennie Mackintosh gable ends and the swimming pool elevation, to the small details of railings.

The Twentieth Century

The first quarter of the twentieth century saw the rise of many specialist shop fitting firms. These firms produced standard lettering for name fascias and window sections and in some cases offered whole shop fronts of tailor made design. Prefabricated shop fronts in cast iron were available from the mid nineteenth century but the twentieth century saw an explosion of change. The wood fronted Edwardian and Victorian shops were swept away in the new desire for a glittering chrome and glass surround in the highly competitive world of shop selling. The result of this was that the streetscapes of major cities lost the order and rhythm of the nineteenth century when the craft of sign maker, metalworker and joiner combined to produce an exciting and human texture at pavement level. Professor C. H. Reilly wrote, in the ARCHITECTURAL REVIEW (Vol. 78, 1935): *A casual glance down Oxford Street, Bond Street, the Western Road, Brighton, or any important provincial thoroughfare lined with shops, is enough to make one wonder whether in this England of ours shops and shop fronts are not altogether outside the pale of the arts. That they may one day, like all other solid static things, be part of an ordered architecture, and not*

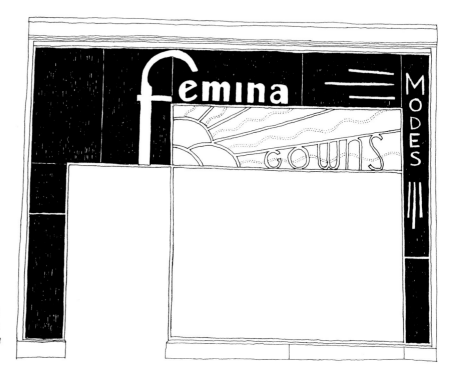

Shop, Wicklow Street, Dublin
The Femina Shop in Wicklow Street was built about 1929 and is one of the many high class designs which were produced by the famous Dublin shopfitting firm of Squires. The design has several Art Deco features although it is in essence an early Irish exercise in the Modern Movement.

merely expressions of disorderly competitive commerce, needs a faith similar in kind at any rate to that which must have moved the Creator of the Universe when He first looked down on chaos.

One wonders what the Professor would say if he looked at the streets today? In the 1920s and right into the 1930s the general standard of craft, at least, was high and the materials used were generally of extremely high quality even if the choice and juxtaposition of materials was often insensitive. The era had arrived when the average life of a shop front was dramatically shortened. This was in line with the new frenzy for change in style and fashion of the goods for sale – the shop front had to reflect these in the same ephemeral manner. Few shop fronts of the 1920s and 1930s now survive in the major cities, although the classical type front which was still being built well into the twentieth century seems to have survived a good deal better.

The Femina shop in Wicklow Street, Dublin was an interesting departure from the classical shop fronts of the early twentieth century so expertly turned out by firms such as Squires. This is the shop front designed with total disregard for its upper parts and its neighbours. The applied skin deep nature is emphasised by the non-articulation of the joints of the black 'Vitrolite' panels and the uniform plane of shop window, frames and panels.

The design is certainly influenced by the De Stijl Movement with its flat interplay of proportions and the use of spotless surfaces. The pioneers of De Stijl would not have approved, however, of the joyful sunburstery or of the surprisingly successful chrome lettering. A photograph of the shop taken shortly after it was built shows this lettering in a different position over the entrance. For some reason the letters were later moved to their present position, the designer possibly perfecting the proportions of the front.

Shop, Westmoreland Street, Dublin Kennedy and McSharry's shop front is a typical shop front of the 1920s. It was designed and fitted by a firm of shop fitters, Pollard Furniture of London. The date of the work was 1929 and the supervisory architect was George O'Connor, the main contractor being Cramptons.
The front is carried out entirely in metal with the lettering in bronze. The design is assured and provides an interesting link between the exuberance of the late nineteenth century and the new asceticism of the Modern Movement.

One of the pioneers of the Modern Movement in Britain was Raymond McGrath (1903–1977) who came to Ireland in 1940 and became Principal Architect of the Office of Public Works. In 1933, A. Trystan Edwards wrote THE ARCHITECTURE OF SHOPS which illustrated many of the shops of the 1920s. In this book the shops of Raymond McGrath, built during the late 1920s, show a definite break from the confused designs of the period and are clearly early Modern Movement. Among his best designs were Easiwork Kitchen Cabinets in Tottenham Court Road, the showrooms of National Flying Services and Imperial Airways and Fishers off Bond Street, which Raymond McGrath considered his best design of the period. Unfortunately all of these shops have long disappeared.

Easiwork Kitchen Cabinets was built in 1930. The design was pure Modern Movement with its interplay of proportions and clear simple surfaces. The gospel of functionalism was preached by the emphasis on the awning as an important feature of the design. The soffit over the shop windows was powerfully curved to suck the customer into the interior. Curiously, decoration was not considered totally unacceptable and a mosaic design in contrasting colours, according to Raymond McGrath, was used to decorate the side panels.

Lochner's Pork Butcher's shop was built in 1948 and the architects were Buckley and O'Gorman. The design, although post war, has many features of early Modern – the porthole, rounded corners and the projecting display window, which has a cleverly integrated venetian blind inside.

Except for a few isolated houses, some hospital work and cinemas built in the 1930s, the Modern Movement only began to make an impact in Ireland after the second World War.

Shop, Tottenham Court Road, London

where the demands of the ship building industry were insatiable in the seventeenth and early eighteenth centuries. In the eighteenth century the wood used for most building work was imported Baltic 'fir' and pine. This was far easier to carve and throughout the nineteenth century in Ireland the joiners and carvers combined to produce an astonishing variety of wood fronted shops.

Entablature

The classical entablature evolved on very sound and practical principles as a building element with each component carefully improved to throw off rain water and to protect the parts of the building below. The entablature with its cornice was an extremely practical finish to the upper parts of a shop front. Aesthetically it finished off the top of the design and protected the shop front from the weather. The frieze was an excellent place for the name of the shop and the proportions of this name panel in relation to the elevation were remarkably constant right up to the first quarter of the twentieth century when the rule was broken with disastrous consequences.

Consoles

Consoles or brackets probably originated from the decorated ends of projecting beams. The standard form of a console is an S-shaped double volute with, in the form used on shops, the large spiral at the top and the small spiral at the bottom. The console was a very convenient way of closing off the ends of the entablature and the nameboard and thus defining the shop from its immediate neighbour. The earlier shop did not use a console to close the design but allowed the cornice to project. This gave problems when the shop front came right up to the frontage of the neighbouring shop. To allow the cornice to have its proper return the frieze was hollowed out as a scotia shape. With wider frontages, and with space to spare, the cornice was always projected at the ends and the frieze, in many simple small town examples, is left plain.

The carved consoles and brackets of Irish shops are a real delight and it is quite remarkable to realise the variety of designs and changes which the skilled craftsmen of the time could ring on this basic element. It is possible to see the same hand throughout on many old shops in Irish towns, but even here the craftsmen will vary the design from one shop to the next.

Pilasters and columns

A flat pilaster formed of wood with a rudimentary cap to keep out the water was the first and obvious way to frame the shop front and support the nameboard. The pilasters of many small shops in country towns have a simple astragal or fillet at the top and with their recessed panels give a peaceful and human rhythm to the village street. The influence of the pattern books with their engravings of the classical orders, brought the full glory of Tuscan, Doric, Ionic and Corinthian to Irish towns. The columns were often very thin and this must have disturbed many a scholar of classical grammar. Mary Eldridge

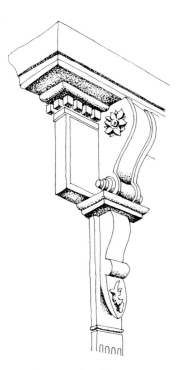

Bracket Detail, Thomastown, Co. Kilkenny
This bracket detail, from a small shop in Thomastown, shows a simplified console with a rosette decoration on the side. This detail is unusual in that the cornice is allowed to project beyond the console. The pilasters also have a very unusual bracket with the end lifted away from the background. The whole shop front is a masterpiece of the small town woodworker's art and craft.

Shop, Monkstown, Co. Dublin
Tyndall's shop is a magnificent wood-fronted shop of late nineteenth-century design. The frieze is without brackets at the ends, which are delightfully carved in a cyma recta shape. For such a small shop the designer's attempt to give the front a gracefully sculptured three dimensional effect is in particular contrast to many of the skin deep modern shop fronts.

quotes from a critic in the WESTMINSTER REVIEW, (October 1841): *thousands of diminutive copies of the same originals are to be seen all over the town, all apparently turned out of the same manufactory – for which reason we wonder that no one should have established one where columns may be purchased ready for use like chimney pots.*

To our less puritanical eyes the little engaged and fluted columns of the small scale Irish shops are a joy. Some towns like Enniscorthy, Co. Wexford, repeat the same little Ionic detail on different shops and the rhythm of the columns can be an easy going discipline and unifying device on the often ragged vernacular of the provincial street.

Shutters

The obvious reason for the use of wooden shutters was security, to prevent theft from the display windows and access to the shop. The Victorian middle class shop keeper was highly security conscious as a photograph of King Street, Manchester, in 1866, in THE VICTORIAN CITY edited by Dyos & Wolff, showed. The view is of a good class shopping street absolutely barricaded for the night with wooden shutters on every shop, most of these being held in place by padlocked flat section iron bars across the lower part. Shutters on shops in Irish cities would have been there for the same reason, but the shutters on shops in small Irish market towns would have also served another purpose. Fair days up to ten or twenty years ago turned most market towns into a riot of animals and people, with the shop windows very vulnerable to excitable bullocks or shying horses. Many towns today still have the old wooden shutters with their neat panelled proportions. They are often brightly painted to liven up the street when the shops are closed.

Shop, Youghal, Co. Cork
John Forrest's shop is in Youghal, a town which has a great number of excellent old shop fronts. The wood shutters are beautifully proportioned and related to the overall shape of the front. This shop is simple in design and the elegant little fanlight is the only lighthearted feature of a strongly robust and expert piece of work.

A nineteenth-century market day in Carrickmacross, Co. Monaghan.

Optician's Shop, Duke Street, Dublin Murray McGrath's shop was built in 1914 and the designer was James Montgomery. The work is a thorough exercise in the art of wood shop fronts. The classical details are all simplified and robust and the design is a nostalgic eighteenth-century revival.

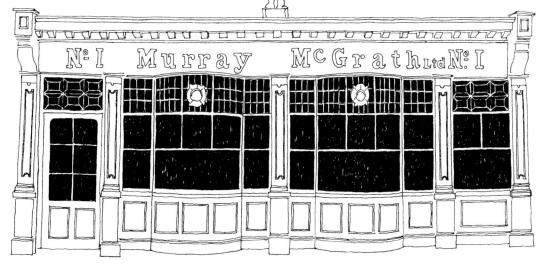

Shop, Thomastown, Co. Kilkenny
O'Murcada's little shop in
Thomastown has many features which
are common on other shops still
existing in the town and pointing to the
work of the same craftsman. The frieze
is closed by curly end pieces in wood
which set off the wooden frill above the
name. The extremely thin round
columns have the simplest of caps and
are typical of many shops in Irish
towns. The windows were almost
certainly divided into smaller lights
when first built.

Shop, Kildorrery, Co. Cork
In this delightful village there are very
many beautifully preserved shop fronts
and several of these are obviously the
work of one master craftsman. The
carved mullions are highly
individualistic and the richly carved
brackets and modillioned cornice
combine to present an extremely exotic
effect.

Shop, Youghal, Co. Cork
Kenneally's little shop is another
example of the many fine old shops in
Youghal. The woodworker indulged
his craft here with a great variety of
classical detail. This included a
nailheaded band across the top of the
cornice and the same device on the
brackets. The exotically shaped
window mullions are exactly
proportioned to take economic sized
panes of glass. The whole front is a
truly Irish craftsman's solution to the
shop front design problem.

Hardware Shop, Cahirciveen, Co.
Kerry
O'Neill's is a very characteristic design
of the mid nineteenth century and there
are many examples of this design
throughout the country. Nineteenth-
century photographs show how
common the narrow round-headed
windows were on little shops in many
towns. In O'Neills the spandrils are
unglazed and are decorated with rich
wood carving. Unfortunately, here, as
in many cases, the detail is almost
obliterated by many layers of paint.
The original windows would have
been divided by a very thin horizontal
rail.

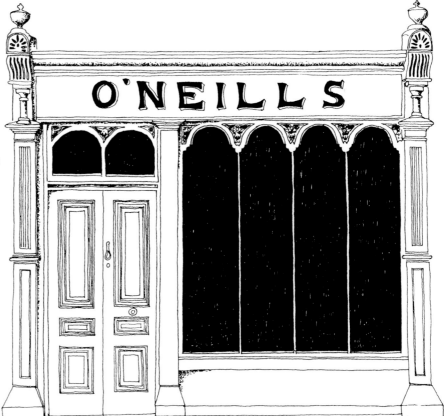

Metal

The first use of metal in shop fronts was almost certainly restricted to the use of iron as hinges and struts for the open counter and bars for the shutters. Iron then came into its own as a decorative material for shop fronts in the late eighteenth and early nineteenth centuries.

Cast Iron

Iron has been used for at least three thousand years and cast iron was used for railings for St Paul's Cathedral in 1714. However, it wasn't until Abraham Darby, at his foundry at Coalbrookdale in Shropshire, perfected the manufacture of iron by using coke instead of charcoal and later the method of casting iron in sand, that cast iron decorative elements became cheap and widely available.

Structural components, particularly cast iron columns, were used quite early in the nineteenth century to free the shop facade and allow large sheets of plate glass to be used for display. The manufacturers of small decorative items, such as railings, balustrading, cast iron frills etc., had eager customers from the small shops of the nineteenth century.

Builders' catalogues of the nineteenth century show a huge variety of standard prefabricated goods available in cast iron. The balustrading along the tops of cornices of shops was commonly in cast iron which was ideal for coupling together in sections. There was tremendous variety in these ranging from thin and elegant railings with floral infills to short frills which softened the flat top of the cornices. Cast iron had good resistance to corrosion and was well suited, even with fairly irregular painting, to outdoor use.

Cast Iron Shop front, Bruff, Co. Limerick
This magnificent example of the prefabricated cast iron shop front is in the little town of Bruff, Co. Limerick. It is a general drapery store and still has the original interiors with many shop fittings intact.
The lettering, cast in with the fascia, is strongly Art Nouveau in character which would date the shop about 1900. The beautiful and delicate iron centrepiece with the little shamrock frills was a common device on the larger shops of country towns and many still exist around the country.

The front was cast in fairly large sections which were bolted together on site with great precision. The technology of the prefabrication and craft of the design and assembly is far in advance of the often shoddy and short lived modern shop fronts of the provinces.

Complete shop fronts prefabricated in cast iron became available in the mid nineteenth century. They arrived as a kit-of-parts, fascia, cornice and window frames which were moulded in with columns or pilasters.

The IRISH BUILDER for 1890 contains advertisements from Walter MacFarlane & Co. of Glasgow for: *Shop fronts wholly or partially of cast iron, suitable for all classes of business – 2 Gold Medals Calcutta Exhibition.* J. McGloughlin & Sons advertised iron, copper and brass.

Wrought Iron

Wrought iron is more ductile than cast iron and historically it was used for structural members in tension. Thomas Telford used wrought iron for the great suspension chains of the Menai road bridge, built in 1819. Wrought iron could be easily forged and therefore is more suitable for decorative and creative craft. It was more expensive than cast iron and not available in standard off-the-peg designs, and its use in shops was confined to the occasional little gate screen to close the shop entrance door. Wrought iron was sometimes combined with cast iron to make up decorative railings but is less corrosion resistant than cast iron and needs to be constantly repainted.

Railing and Lamp standard, A.P.C.K. Bookshop, Dawson St., Dublin
When shops were set back from their original building line, the territorial imperative made owners anxious to define their own area. The lamp standard is of the high quality for which the street lighting fixtures of Dublin are renowned.
The rather fearsome character of the iron railing may have been inspired by Art Nouveau.

Copper Bronze Brass

The non-ferrous metals were always much more expensive than iron or steel and their use was confined to detail work or for places where resistance to corrosion was paramount.

Copper on shop fronts was mainly decorative as it was capable of being worked with intricate designs as in Crymbles Music Shop in Belfast. Bronze is an alloy of copper with tin and is ideal for casting into intricate shapes. The more expensive door furniture was usually bronze and in shop fitting it was used in extruded form for window frames. A description of Walpoles newly opened shop in Wicklow Street, Dublin in the IRISH BUILDER for 14 January 1905 describes window sashes by Stanley Jones & Co. made of gun metal which 'oxidises to a beautiful even tone and will require no polishing or cleaning.' There is a photograph of this shop which was designed by Charles Ashworth and built by J. & P. Good.

Brasses are alloys of copper and their ability to take a high polish made them ideal for decorative work in shops. Many Irish shops and pubs had brass rails outside across the window for the dual purpose of protecting the glass and to prevent the practice, very prevalent in the nineteenth century as evidenced by contemporary photographs, of sitting and lounging on the window sills to watch the world go by.

Undertaker, Youghal, Co. Cork
The sombre character of the cast iron
frill on top of the cornice of Egan's
shop front may be in keeping with the
solemn nature of the business.
Although hardly a joyous shop front, it
is nevertheless an excellent piece of
craftwork and a credit to its designers.

Glass

The glass used in early Georgian times, when shops first began to glaze the fronts, was almost certainly crown glass. The glass was blown into a bubble by the glass maker and then spun and while still molten beaten into a flat sheet up to about 1200mm in diameter. The panes which were cut from these were quite small. Raymond McGrath in GLASS IN ARCHITECTURE describes a shop formerly in Limehouse and dating from about 1800 where the panes were twenty-two and a quarter inches by fifteen and a quarter inches. An interesting feature of this shop window was the curved end made from narrow vertical panes of glass. Plate glass appeared at the end of the eighteenth century; made from a cylinder rather than a bubble and being of a greater thickness throughout it could be ground and polished. The new plate glass was obviously an exciting arrival on the building scene. Peter Nicholson in THE PRACTICAL BUILDER (1823)

commenting on the 'qualities of plate glass' gives a lyrical and almost poetic description of the material: *The qualities of this glass are conspicuous to persons accustomed to examine the goodness of materials, and, in many instances, must be apparent to the common observer. The best description is recognised for its clearness as well as richness, and it is also free from the peculiar redness adverted to, which approximates to the colour of scarlet water, made by lake, and which, on being mixed or diluted in clear cold spring water, resembles the blushing faded rose.*

Shop, Youghal, Co. Cork
In this shop the economic glass size dictated the entire window design. The horizontal glazing bar was kept extremely thin to allow the essential vertical proportions to dominate. The woodcarver made a bulb at the meeting with the mullions, which themselves were rounded and shaped to reduce their apparent thickness. There are many existing shops of this design particularly in Youghal and other small towns in Co. Cork and Co. Kerry.

Chandler & Hardware Shop, Sandymount, Dublin
Sandymount Stores, built at the turn of the century, is one of the most beautifully preserved shops in Ireland. The interior is intact and the shop is being preserved by its enthusiastic owners. The curved plate glass here is a very fine feature which makes the little shop with its richly decorated detail a real jewel of townscape adjoining Sandymount Green. The classical details have an Art Nouveau exuberance about them.

Plate glass was unfortunately very expensive and until a thinner and cheaper form was introduced it made only a very slow impact on shop windows. J. Young's book DESIGNS FOR SHOP FRONTS published in 1830 shows panes of glass of an average length of only four feet and this size remained fairly constant often up to the end of the nineteenth century in Ireland. The reasons for the small size were obviously economy, ease of transport and fitting, but aesthetic considerations cannot be ruled out since many commentators of the time disliked the sight of masonry which appeared to sit uncomfortably on large sheets of glass.

Mary Eldridge commented that even though the excise duty on glass was repealed in 1845 and in 1852 the largest size obtainable was eight feet by fourteen feet, the usual size was a vertical strip seven to eight feet by three to four feet. She arrived at this conclusion by measuring quite a number of existing old shops. The use of glass in these strips gave a strong vertical emphasis to shop fronts and became a major design generator and discipline. Many of the nineteenth-century shops as illustrated in this book have had their vertical glazing bars and probably the round heads and decorative spandrils removed in modern times and have been reglazed with large sheets of polished plate glass. The results are almost always unsympathetic to the scale of the shop front and of the street. An early description of the use of plate glass in Ireland appears in the DUBLIN BUILDER of 1 June 1859. There is a report on the opening of new premises for Telfords of Henry Street, 'which contained two of the largest sheets of plate glass in Dublin.' Raymond McGrath in GLASS IN ARCHITECTURE commenting on the slow acceptance of very large sheets of glass stated: '*A sensibility to good architectural scale restrained the shopkeeper – a restraint nowhere better exemplified than in the Parisian fronts of Le Style Empire, an elegant example of which – No. 21 Rue du Faubourg Saint-Honore, Paris – is illustrated*' [*in* GLASS IN ARCHITECTURE *(88) 229*].

The arrival of moulded or curved plate glass in the later part of the nineteenth century made the first significant change in shop planning possible for many years. Mary Eldridge considered that 1859 saw one

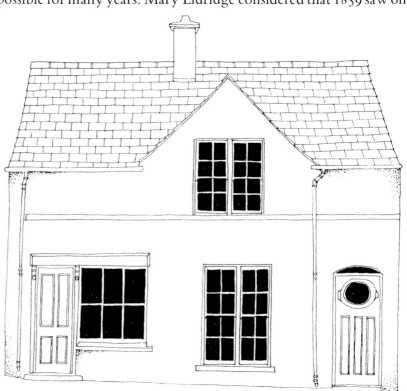

House and Shop, Dungiven, Co. Londonderry
The traditional use of the small pane of glass in Georgian proportions lived on in Ireland for many years. In this little shop in Dungiven the simple shop window has kept the same proportions as the Georgian panes in the sash windows of the house. Very many of these shops are no longer used as such, but the owners retain the shopfront and window and in some cases even the nameboard, thus keeping a landmark and a link with history.

of the earliest uses of moulded plate glass in a shop with moulded bow windows in Law's shop 102 New Oxford Street, London.

The curved plate glass made fully glazed corners possible with the structural supports free of glass framing and placed behind the window. They also made possible the continuation of the window display on either side of the entrance doors which could be very deeply recessed. Window shopping indeed arrived in a big way with the large under cover display windows.

Up to the time of the development of the multiple stores and the cheap department stores, shopping, except for the rich, could have been an intimidating experience. The early shops did not bother with interesting window displays or with such trivialities as marked prices and the rich in the Georgian period simply browsed for hours in the shops and bought their goods on account. The poor bargained from the street traders and small unglazed shops.

From the 1870s onwards, multiple stores and Department Stores founded by men like Thomas Lipton, Jesse Boot and later Woolworths and Marks & Spencers' Penny Bazaars, were to cash in on the desire of the middle and lower class workers to shop in security and see the goods which were available and to know the exact price. The windows of the first multiple shops were a riot of information and offered an extraordinary number of choices. The very large sheets of plate glass did not appear in shop windows until after 1860 and in Ireland the multiple stores like Findlaters, Maypole Dairies, Tylers, Liptons and others would have certainly been among the first major users of the large sheet.

Shop, Galway City
This fine draper's shop is a perfectly preserved early twentieth century example of the attractive stores of provincial towns. The curved glass windows allowed window shopping in *shelter and a larger display area. The lettering is very fine. The letters are carved into the background which is painted green, with gold for the chamfered letters, and the fascia is then covered with plate glass.*

65

Plaster

The greatest building tradition of Ireland was in the use of stone, a tradition that began several thousand years ago in the great monuments of the Neolithic Era. Building stones, however, needed to be carefully selected from the best quarries for good quality building and this was not always possible or economic for the buildings of the ordinary people. Rain, driven hard by high winds, penetrated even a well built wall of good material and many walls were plastered to make them weatherproof. The plaster used was a mixture of lime, mortar and sand gauged with cement to form easily applied and easily moulded layers.

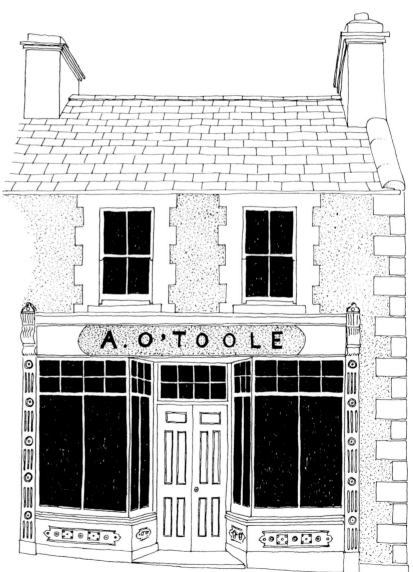

Shop, Louisburgh, Co. Mayo
The house is decorated in a manner very common throughout Ireland – the quoins and windows are emphasised in plaster in the old stone tradition and the background is, in this case, pebble dashed. In many parts these different elements would then be colour washed in contrasting shades.
The shop front has been given the full treatment. The woodcarving tradition is not so strong in the West, but the desire for decoration, for individuality and the joy of craft, is expressed in the delightfully simple plaster designs.

Old Shop, Annascaul, Co. Kerry
This house has retained the name panel over the former shop window, although the use as a shop has long ceased. The plaster letters and panel were the work of a local plasterer about 1900 and it is likely that he was influenced by the powerful presence of Pat McAuliffe. The little hand motif appears in a few places in Co. Kerry pointing at the name in the same way as McAuliffe's arrows point at 'O'Mara' in Abbeyfeale. Other little plaster motifs on name boards are common in Castleisland, Co. Kerry. Although the lettering itself is crude, its unsophistication is part of the wild and natural landscape of the Dingle peninsula.

Plaster Bracket Detail, Killorglin, Co. Kerry

Exterior plastering or stucco, as it was known, was used by Palladio. It was later commonly used by classical revival architects for dressing up buildings in inferior walling materials to make them look like stone palaces.

Peter Nicholson in THE PRACTICAL BUILDER (1823) gave a specification for stucco giving Roman cement mixed with equal parts of 'clean sharp grit sand' and then went on to say that 'In Ireland, where the lime is many degrees superior to the English, the architects prefer their own country lime to our Roman cement . . .'.

The material had many attractions for the builder in country areas when he tackled the problem of the small house and shop front. With plaster he could imitate all sorts of classical detailing particularly dressy window surrounds and decorative quoins and string courses.

For the shop front itself it was possible to produce an entire classical front consisting of entablature with flanking pilasters or engaged columns all in plaster, thus saving time and the expense of good quality stone.

The strongest tradition of exterior decoration in plaster is in the south western part of Ireland. The most famous plasterworker-designer whose work is still to be seen in many parts of Co. Kerry was Pat McAuliffe (1846–1921). Listowel, Co. Kerry was the town where most of McAuliffe's work was carried out, but there is some excellent work in Abbeyfeale, Co. Limerick.

67

McAuliffe's work was cast in cement and sand from a mould made in local blue clay. James Quirke of Abbeyfeale, who was a plasterer following in McAuliffe's tradition and whose father knew McAuliffe, said that McAuliffe had old cast iron ornaments from which he made impressions for casting.

The intricate work would have been vibrated by hand before being fixed to the facade.

McAuliffe's work, particularly his excellent lettering which is highly individual and innovatory, shows strong influences of Art Nouveau. He has often been described, or rather dismissed, as a naive artist, but there are features about his work which show him to be a genuine designer working in the new exotic and exciting decorative phase of the late nineteenth century. His figure work is the least successful but is the work which attracts most notice and most of the many stories about this unusual man. His decorations on buildings were often rather out of scale but there is no denying his genuine desire to turn ordinary dull town buildings into sculptural and textural art objects.

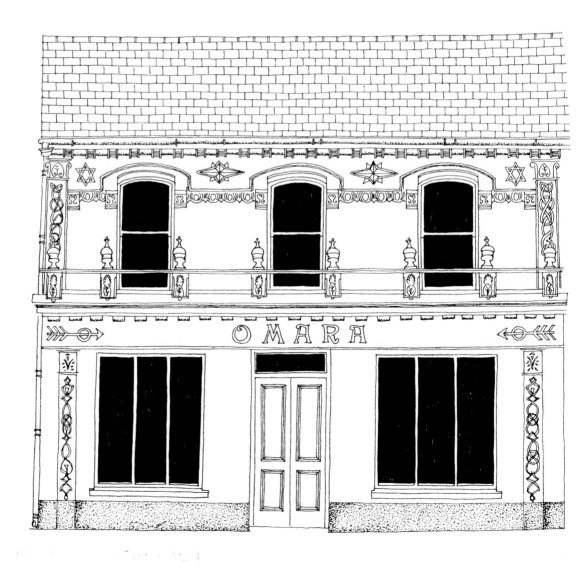

House, Pub, Abbeyfeale, Co. Limerick
Pat McAuliffe was at his best when he was allowed to completely decorate a whole house front. In this example he mixed classical detail with his own motifs with great success. The egg and dart ovolo band linking the windows is an original and delightfully sculptural feature and is much larger than it should be according to classical principles. The interlaced decorations and the high relief motifs are a typically curious mixture of Celtic and Middle East influences.

Shop and House, Abbeyfeale, Co. Limerick

This is one of Pat McAuliffe's most dramatic designs, although some of its original details have been removed. An elaborate balustrade in concrete finishing off the cornice was removed in the 1930s, as its top-heaviness was considered a danger to people in the street. The lettering is modern and the original shop, which was a bar and grocer's, would almost certainly have had the individualistic McAuliffe lettering. In this design McAuliffe's enthusiasm to demonstrate as much variety of design as possible broke the classical rules, with rather fascinating results. The diamond-pointed rustication which graced the top storey would have been more appropriately carried down to the shop front cornice in the traditional Irish manner. McAuliffe, however, introduced his own special brand of flat, incised, pilasters to create no less than three different vertical layers.

Tiles

In the nineteenth century the Arts and Crafts movement and its founder William Morris endeavoured to recreate the old close relationship between the artist and the craftsman. Alongside this elite movement the voracious technology and expansionism of Victorian industry was making a mass produced aesthetic available to all. More than any other new product glazed tiles became synonymous with Victorian high flown decoration. Faience, as the tiles for exterior use on walls were known, is a form of glazed stoneware or terracotta. Victorian manufacturers produced many catalogues showing the enormous range available. Butchers' shops, dairies and fishmongers were the main shops to use tiles for the obvious reasons of hygiene and to produce a clean attractive appearance.

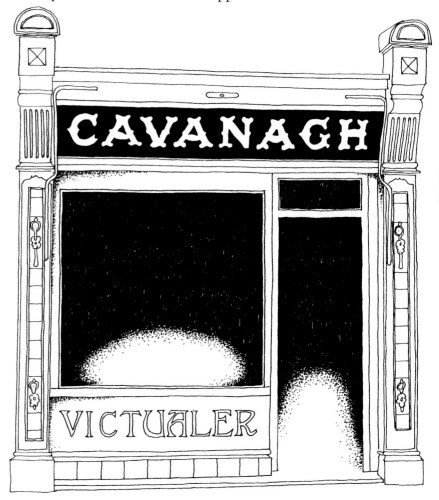

Butcher's Shop, Sligo
This little shop is clad with glazed tiles around the display window and up to the robustly carved wood brackets. There are brightly coloured floral decorations on the pilasters and the stylish lettering on large tiles under the window is simplified Art Nouveau. The term 'Victualler' is one of the many euphemisms used for trading purposes. In the Northern part of the country, a butcher's shop is known as a 'flesher' which is perhaps more exact, if not picturesque.

The glazed tiles could be handpainted or transfer-printed to any design required but towards the end of the nineteenth century the really exotic Victorian invention was 'Majolica Ware'. These tiles had heavily sculptured shapes rising above the surface and they were usually in rich or bright colours.

The firm of Doultons of Lambeth was one of the major firms in the ceramics business and they were joined in 1890 by W. J. Neatby who took charge of architectural ceramics. J. Barnard, who has researched the work of Neatby and ceramic tiles, has written several interesting articles on the work of this great designer (see bibliography) and commented: *The use of ceramic tiles for cladding a building was by no means unknown but previously for technical reasons, the glazes were always a drab yellow brown. Developments at Doultons had produced glazes that enabled the artist to use any colours without fear of deterioration from weathers.*

Sadly the vast majority of these splendid faience decorated shops have disappeared. Only a very few remain in Ireland, although sometimes fragments of what was once a splendid design can be found partially covered by modern plastic and hardboard. A few interiors of butchers' shops survive, decorated usually with pastoral scenes and contradicting the gory nature of the business.

Shop, Ardee, Co. Louth
Hamill's is a tour de force of faience majolica. The tiles are in two shades of green with a light background. The dainty festoons of flowers and leaves interlacing the splendid Art Nouveau lettering are the most striking features of one of the best shop fronts in the country. Apart from the fact that this front is one of the last survivors of a remarkable period in the history of shop design, Hamill's deserves to be preserved and cherished for its contribution to the townscape of Ardee. The shop was originally a grocery with a pub, which was a common combination in the provincial centres and small towns. The tiling would have been a cheerful and hygienic surround to large blocks of yellow butter and sides of bacon.

Signs and Paint

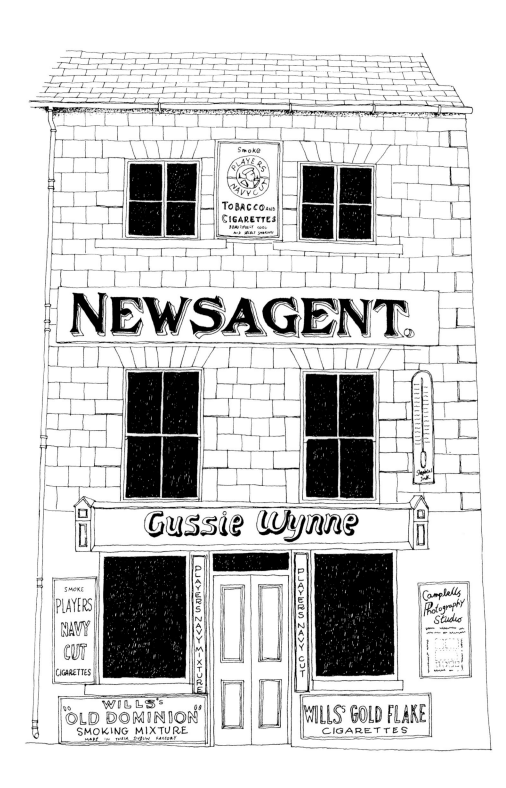

Irish shopfronts make their most individual and vital contribution to the street scene in the art of hand painted lettering. This work was generally carried out by a local craftsman whose particular style can sometimes be seen throughout an entire town or region. Some of the signpainters were adept at all styles of lettering and others stuck firmly to a well practised face.

The alphabets were almost always serifed and when sanserif letters were used it was usually the work of an inexpert signwriter or the letters were cut out and fixed on the fascia.

Shadowed lettering was one of the most favoured forms and the shadows were usually separated by a thin space from the body of the letters to give a finely three dimensional form. An interesting variation, examples of which can be seen in Birr and in Wexford, was to put the shadows on top of the letters as if the name was lit from below. This was particularly effective in a narrow street.

Family names are almost universally used on shop fronts. Although sixteenth and seventeenth-century Dublin had premises with names like the 'Three Wolves Head', the provinces never followed suit to any great extent. There is however, a strong tradition of retaining the original name on the shop front even when the business has changed hands many times. A shop in Enniscorthy has the name of the original owner from the time the shop first changed hands in 1890. The name of the shop becomes a signpost and a link with history in the manner of a grove of trees or a cairn of stones in a long inhabited landscape.

Another lettering tradition which developed in the late nineteenth century was almost certainly initiated on high class shops whose owners desired a prestige name fascia. This technique involved cutting the letters deeply into a wood background which was painted, with the incised and chamfered letters picked out in gold.

Shop, Castlebar, Co. Mayo
This building is a veritable architectural billboard in the brash and brazen manner of the high Victorian commercial world.
The splendidly gaunt stone building, typical of one of the best features of Castlebar, is really used only as a backdrop to the advertisements. The large letters 'Newsagent' are painted on to a plastered background and are a fine example of the signwriter's skill. Note the cigarette advertisements made in special vertical narrow panels to fit on nineteenth-century shop pilasters. Old tobacco advertisements did not wish to make parallels with either sex or the virile outdoors. 'Beautifully cool and select smoking' and 'made at their Dublin factory' seemed to be safe enough claims.

Shop, Westport, Co. Mayo
Salmon's little shop is an unchanged fragment of late nineteenth-century Westport, and is now sadly disused and unloved. Re-opened and re-painted it could be a great attraction in this lovely town.

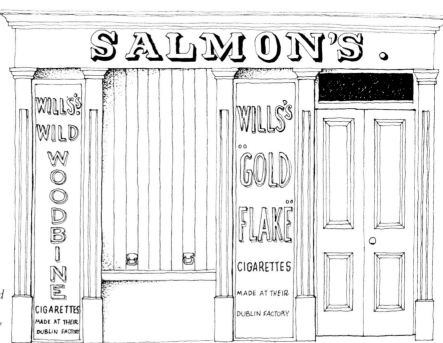

T. McALLISTER

H. GRAHAM

HARDWARE

DRAPERY

AND

AND

GROCERY

BOOTS

The fascia was then covered in plate glass. In Ireland, even quite small shops used this method and small local sign making firms were to be found all over the country. A detailed description of this type of fascia is given in MODERN SHOPFRONT CONSTRUCTION (1949) by Trevor Perry. (See bibliography).

The advertisements which often remain on old shop fronts or higher up on the residential parts of the house, are a fascinating window on the past. Historically the late Victorian period saw the birth of ballyhoo advertising. Photographs taken in the later part of the nineteenth century reveal the kind of goods advertised and the publicity it was felt they needed. A photograph reproduced in THE VICTORIAN CITY (1973) edited by Dyos & Wolff, shows a dairy shop in Liverpool about 1890 with a sign in huge bold lettering: 'Our sixpenny lump is equal in flavour to Fine Irish Butter'. Another photograph shows the Kodak Company head office in Clerkenwell Road about 1902. Apart from one huge storey-high sign, the name 'Kodak' is repeated on smaller signs nearly fifty times. This was very common in Victorian cities where buildings were sometimes almost completely covered by advertisements. The windows of shops and the buildings overhead may have been clamorous with messages, but the quality of the lettering was almost always good. Irish provincial towns appeared to have a good deal less advertising than cities like Dublin, Belfast and Cork, but it is still possible to see large faded painted signs high up on provincial buildings.

The metal stove enamelled signs advertising tobacco, dyes, pet foods, boot polish, etc., can often still be seen, resplendent in their bright colours and virile lettering.

Up to the later eighteenth century, city shops were identified by hanging signs over the front, rather than by the name of the proprietor. The signs became large and elaborate and developed from the simpler painted signs of the seventeenth century, into large

symbols carved and gilded in the eighteenth century. A contemporary writer describes the signs in London as: *Very large, very fine, and very absurd, golden periwigs, saws, axes, lancets, razors, trees, knives, salmon, cheeses, black's heads, half moons, sugar loaves and Westphalian hams. . . .*

By 1762 the authorities had decided that the signs must be controlled as they constituted a danger, dripped water and creaked noisily in the wind.

The DUBLIN BUILDER of 1 November 1864 carried in its leading article a strong attack on the bureaucratic 'Corporate authorities' who insisted on signs being removed from shops: *We are at a loss to understand what useful purpose can be served by a crusade against the time honoured, once universal custom of indicating to the public by a projecting sign the nature of the trade, calling or occupation of the owner who dwelt under its shadow.* The same issue of the DUBLIN BUILDER carried a letter from an 'Edgar Adolphe' who was a photographer in Grafton Street complaining that the Corporation made him remove a sign of a 'Golden Palette, which cost him five pounds', from over his premises.

Barber's Shop, Dungarvan, Co. Waterford
Sometimes rather sad fragments of fine old shops can be detected behind cheap plywood and plastic modern fronts, but here in this little barber's shop in Dungarvan, the honestly robust tradition of signpainting can still give dignity to the 'relics of old dacency'. The lettering recognises the architectural syntax instead of mutilating it in the modern manner.

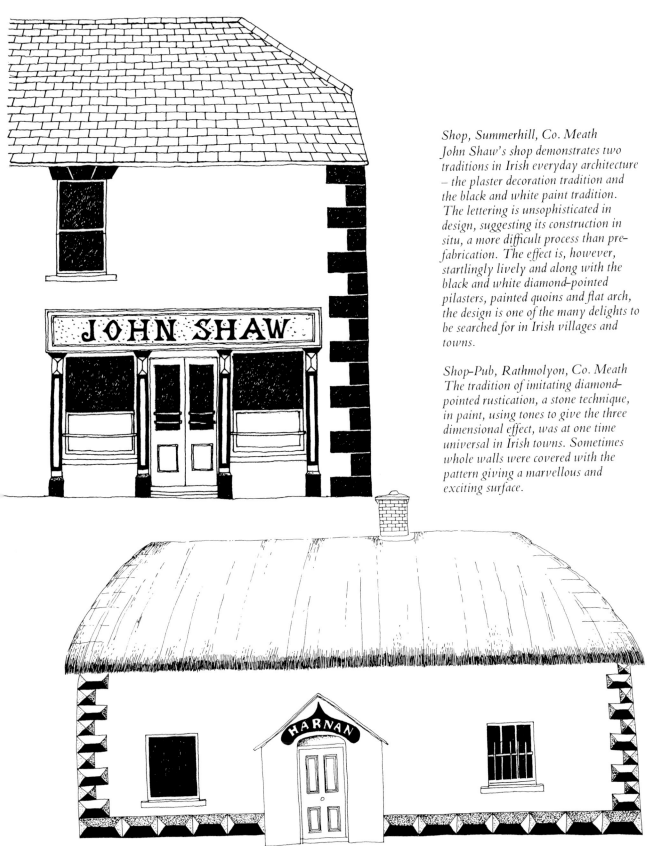

Shop, Summerhill, Co. Meath
John Shaw's shop demonstrates two traditions in Irish everyday architecture – the plaster decoration tradition and the black and white paint tradition. The lettering is unsophisticated in design, suggesting its construction in situ, a more difficult process than pre-fabrication. The effect is, however, startlingly lively and along with the black and white diamond-pointed pilasters, painted quoins and flat arch, the design is one of the many delights to be searched for in Irish villages and towns.

Shop-Pub, Rathmolyon, Co. Meath
The tradition of imitating diamond-pointed rustication, a stone technique, in paint, using tones to give the three dimensional effect, was at one time universal in Irish towns. Sometimes whole walls were covered with the pattern giving a marvellous and exciting surface.

From the eighteenth century onwards, when the cheaper and more vulnerable Baltic softwoods replaced native oak, the painting of woodwork became essential. Protection of the wood and decoration went hand in hand and white lead was the main ingredient of paint in the eighteenth century.

Shop, Convoy, Co. Donegal
The natural reluctance of Irish people in country districts to knock down old buildings which might be useful for some future purpose was, at least until recent years, a bonus to the interested traveller from outside the district. The history of the area could be seen and studied in the remains of cottages and farm buildings, old walls and gates. The old signs on shops are a nostalgic reminder of the time when the purchase of items like strong boots was one of the most important purchases a country person could make.

Trade demarcation disputes appear to have had an early history. In 1677 the CALENDAR OF ANCIENT RECORDS OF DUBLIN (Vol. V) 146 reported that plasterers were to be: *Prohibited from laying any manner of colours or paintings and are directed to use only whiting, blacking, red lead, red oker, yellow oker, and russet mingled with size only and not with oyle on paine of five pounds for every offense . . . painting or laying colours in oyle . . . was to be reserved for . . . Corporation of Painter Stainers . . .*

Over the years many old shop fronts with mullions, spandrils and consoles carved richly in wood have become almost totally obscured with many layers of paint which has spoiled the original fine craftwork. If the layers of paint were removed some surprisingly fine work would be revealed to the benefit of the shop and the town.

The tradition of painting the shop front in strong bright colours is still very much alive and some small towns like Ennistymon, Co. Clare provide rare panoramas of contrasting colours and a lively rhythm of shapes and planes of a truly human scale. The painting of plastered house fronts is a continuation of the tradition and although the commonest method is to use cement colour washes it is not unusual to see an entire house front and gables painted in oil paint using deep and rich colours of green, violet, purple, red browns, chrome yellows, terra cotta, mustard and crimson.

Shop, Dungannon, Co. Tyrone
The lettering on this shop is of a very high quality and the shapes are delightfully echoed in the wood fretted frills of the cornice. The indulgence in decoration is continued in the plaster decorated window surrounds and cornices, and the building is strongly articulated in the very Irish manner by the raised quoins on each side. The windows in the drawing are a conjectural reconstruction since the shop was damaged recently by bombing. The whole composition is a fine example of the superb Irish heritage of shop-house design.

Pub-Shop, Ennistymon, Co. Clare

Nineteenth-century shops in Main Street, Carrick-on-Suir

Butcher, Flesher, Victualler

Butcher's Shop, Castlepollard, Co. Westmeath
The fair green at Castlepollard is enclosed by very pleasant sets of small scale buildings, giving a real sense of place. Halligan's victualler's shop is painted a cheerful yellow with bright red panels on the pilasters and is an excellent example of unselfconscious good design. Note the old meat rail fixed along the top of the windows and the rail across the lower part of the display window to prevent sitting on the window sill.

The earliest butchers' shops were related to slaughter houses, either directly behind the premises or serving a number of shops nearby. Cattle and sheep were driven in from the country, often through the principal streets, to be slaughtered in primitive conditions and the meat sold directly to the customer. The herds and flocks might be driven great distances and the beasts were often not in the best condition when they arrived in the city. This practice was carried on in major cities up to quite recent times and modern traffic problems and modern marketing methods helped to put a stop to the great cattle and sheep drives which had lasted for centuries. The Smithfield Market in London was served by herds of cattle driven from as far away as the Highlands of Scotland. Cattle were also kept within the city itself, both for meat and, more essentially, for milk. Gardens at the back of town houses served as byres and fodder was obtained from the haymarket. Pigs were a very essential part of the city's economy. Early volumes of the CALENDAR OF ANCIENT RECORDS OF DUBLIN refer to the nuisance caused by swine allowed to roam untended and to forage in the streets of the city.

The state of the city's streets and the need for a new cattle market, planned for North Circular Road, Dublin, was certainly of great concern to the Corporation of the time. The IRISH BUILDER of 1 February 1872 printed a report from the City Engineer: *There are 106 slaughter houses in Dublin the greater number being of the worst and most disgusting description, and located in confined and unwholesome places.*

The earliest butchers' shops were open fronted and merely acted as quick sale outlets for a produce which was highly perishable. Early engravings show the meat carcasses hanging from rails outside over the shop entrance and this practice persisted and indeed was tolerated until modern times. The streets were certainly now paved and cleaner than in mediaeval times, but the practice of exposing meat for sale was an interesting survival from the past. Many nineteenth-century photographs show butchers' shops with extraordinary displays of carcasses hanging across the shop front. These photographs usually also show the butchers' assistants lined up for the picture, and it is possible that an extra large show of carcasses was put on specially for the photograph. THE BOOK OF DUBLIN, published by the Corporation of Dublin in 1929, has an advertisement from Michael McDonough & Co., Victuallers, of Chatham Street, which shows a photograph of their premises with a grand display of hanging carcasses. The advertisement states: *By special Appointment to His Excellency the Governor-General and the Officer's Messes throughout Ireland.*

In the Northern half of the country butcher's shops are known as 'fleshers', while 'victualler' is the more favoured term in the South.

Shop, Kingsgate Street, Coleraine, Co. Londonderry
This beautiful shop is described in the Ulster Architectural Heritage Society's list of Coleraine Buildings: 'A splendid Edwardian shop with bow-fronted glass and large square fluted pillars and pilasters with obelisked brackets. Attractive interior tiling.' The same list reproduces elevations of Coleraine in 1816 from the BOOK OF COLERAINE sketched by an 'unknown hand', which show Georgian shops with bow fronts as well as many simple small pane windows with fascia boards.

Butcher's Shop, Birr, Co. Offaly
Many butchers' shops in country towns are painted white, which helps to give the fronts an individuality and a contrast to the bright colours of other shops. This beautifully kept shop has splendid top shadowed lettering of exceptional quality. The little double wood consoles of the fascia are an interesting variation of the bracket type. Note the ventilators over the window which are characteristic of butchers' shops. A more sophisticated form of ventilation to prevent condensation making the display in the window invisible was advocated in the late nineteenth century. This method placed ventilators under the window sill, allowing air to circulate up the inside of the window and escape at the top.

Shop, Cork City
*Mackey's elegant little shop is not
particularly typical of butchers' shops.
The delicate wood carving and
elaborate detail on such a small shop
exemplifies the care and concern of the
craftsmen to produce good and
satisfactory design on quite ordinary
and humble buildings.*

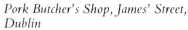

*Shop and House, Mhuinebheag, Co.
Carlow*
*Hatton's shop and house is an exercise
in the 'picturesque' revival styles which
were very popular in the nineteenth
century for estate cottages and estate
villages, in Ireland as well as in
England.*

*Pork Butcher's Shop, James' Street,
Dublin*
*Quinn's shop is one of a series of
similar small shops with standard
fascias linked together by double
pilasters and pediments. The flat bar
meat rail is still in position and the
series of shops is typical of the high
standard of developers' shops and
houses of the late nineteenth and early
twentieth centuries.*

Chemist

The apothecary of old collected or grew his own herbs and many of these men became famous botanists. John Gerarde published his HERBALL in 1597 and William Curtis (1746–1799) practised as an apothecary in London before producing his FLORA LONDINENSIS and the BOTANICAL MAGAZINE. The early pharmacist had only herbs to make his drugs and medicines and the pestle and mortar became the sign of the pharmacist's shop. The sign appears over shops in old engravings of street scenes and persisted until modern times. A chemist's shop in Delvin, Co. Meath still has a crude pestle and mortar motif in plaster over the shop front.

The JOURNAL OF THE CORK HISTORICAL AND ARCHAEOLOGICAL SOCIETY of 1894 contained an item headed 'The first public

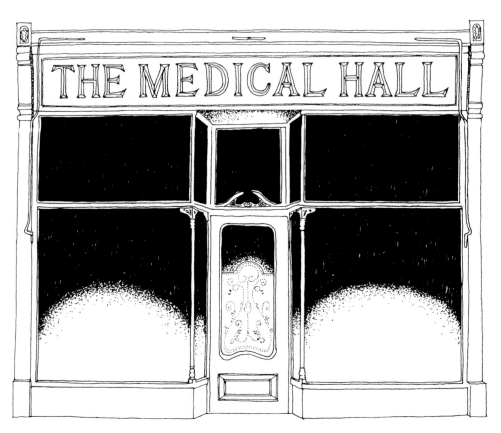

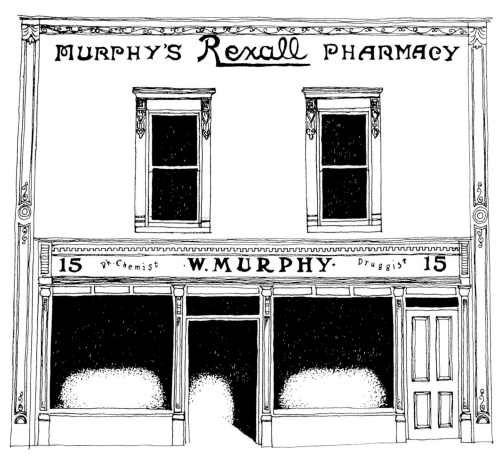

Chemist's Shop, Mitchelstown, Co. Cork
Murphy's chemist's shop is one of the best of many magnificent house-shop fronts in the splendid main street of Mitchelstown. Although several shop fronts have now been mutilated, most of the house fronts over the shops are grandly decorated in plaster designs and colour washed. Murphy's has rather unusual decorated pilasters carried up to eaves level and joined by a little frilly band, also in plaster. The windows on the first floor with their decorative surrounds and cornices are beautifully placed over the extremely neat shop front. The lettering at the top of the building is characteristic of the turn of the century and its quality of design, in comparison with most modern efforts, is a credit to its craftsman.

apothecaries in Cork and Youghal'. In 1626 the Corporation of Youghal: *permitted Thomas Adams, gent., practitioner in the faculty of physicke, to keep an apothecary's shop in their town, first, because he married a freeman's wife (widow?); and secondly, because there was no apothecary in the town.* In the country districts self help was practised and country people became experts on the herbs suitable for medicinal purposes. Hawkers toured the countryside selling and trading all manner of goods and travelling herbalists and medical quacks were also plentiful, selling from door to door or setting up in town markets. Pamela Horn in LABOURING LIFE IN THE VICTORIAN COUNTRYSIDE mentioned the homely remedies which were used by country people such as: 'salts and senna, brimstone and treacle'. She also noted that by the 1870s simple medicines were stocked by the workhouses and unions, particularly stocks of cod liver oil.

The flowering of the chemist's shop as a definite type with its own particular character was a late nineteenth-century happening. John Betjeman describes in ENGLISH CITIES & SMALL TOWNS the chemist shop he remembers: *Rows of little wooden drawers with the names of their contents in black lettering on a gold background, above them old round jars with similar lettering and in the window the big coloured glass bottles of the last century.* Many of the little chemists' shops which date from the 1890s onwards grandly called themselves 'The Medical Hall'. This was in line with the newly discovered world of advertisement and display in the late nineteenth century.

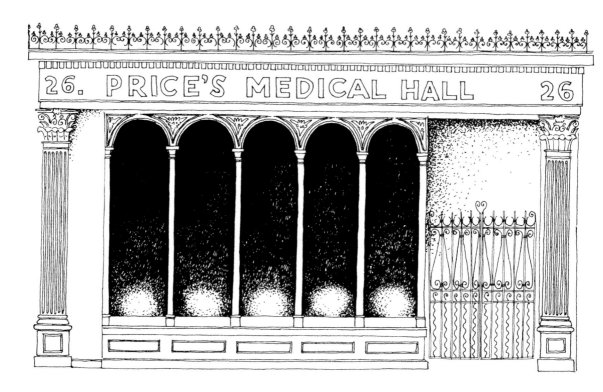

Chemist's Shop, Kilkenny
This is a perfect example of the type of high class shop front produced about 1900. The large plate glass display window which was very fashionable at the time is softened by the Arts and Crafts movement decorative leaded glass over the window and in the door panels. The whole shop front is perfectly preserved and is one of many fine shop fronts surviving and cared for in Kilkenny. (Above left)

Chemist's Shop, Omagh, Co. Tyrone
The curved corner pieces between mullions and transom served a dual purpose. They were primarily structural, allowing a tight and secure joint between the transom and the elegantly thin mullion, but they were also a design device to soften the otherwise hard edge of the window angles. (Above)

Chemist's Shop,
Patrick's Street, Cork
Although Fielding's Pharmacy is hardly earlier than late nineteenth century, the design is curiously eighteenth century in feeling, particularly in the lettering on the plinth. A pretty little shop, which would be very much improved if hand painted lettering replaced the inappropriate sign at present on the fascia. (Below)

Chemist's Shop, Clare Street, Dublin
This is one of the most beautiful and best preserved shop fronts remaining in Dublin. The date is late nineteenth century, but like many other buildings of the period in Ireland, the earlier classical style persists. The windows are slightly bow fronted in eighteenth-century style and the spandrils between the window arches are wood carved. The simplified classical entablature is crowned with a lovely iron frill and is held up by richly decorated corinthian pilasters. (Left)

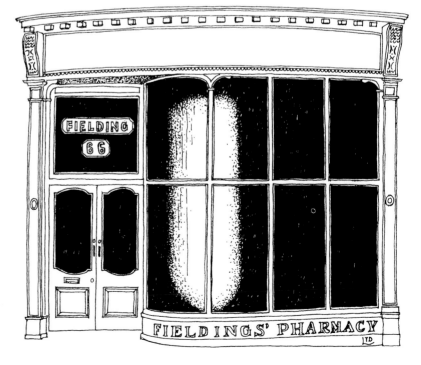

Grocer and General Store

The typical Irish shop in rural areas sells almost everything. The idea of the general store is universal, all the needs of a farming community can be satisfied in one shop. Grocery and provisions are probably the most basic need and when the poverty and concomitant self-sufficiency of Irish country people in the eighteenth and the earlier part of the nineteenth century gave way to easier conditions in the late nineteenth century, the demand for a wider variety of foodstuffs and for luxuries grew. In the cities the demand for a wide variety of food also coincided with increased public health awareness where the sale of food was concerned. The DUBLIN BUILDER of 1 February 1860 printed an article attacking the state of the city markets and advocating new properly designed buildings for the trade, describing the old markets thus: *The huddled shambles of the Coles Lane, the Moore, Leinster or William Street food depots, where man and beast are alike regarded, where the dainty requirements of the one are indiscriminately mixed with the offal thrown to the others, where purchasers nasal organs are at certain seasons submitted to an intolerable test – where in warm weather, from the putrid stores within poisonous exhalations are emitted. . . .*

The new foods which became cheap and available due to late nineteenth-century enterprise were mainly imported and this led to the growth of the multiple shops where a new breed of entrepreneur shopkeepers bought food in bulk and sold cheaply through a chain of outlet shops. One of the first of these in Britain in the food business was Thomas Lipton who opened his first shop in Glasgow in 1872. He imported some of his food supplies in bulk from Ireland which

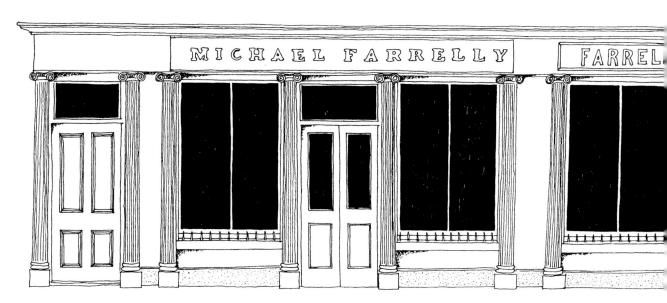

Shop, Westport, Co. Mayo
Kilcoyne's is one of many fine old shop fronts still surviving in this beautiful town and which help in no small way to give the town its exciting and vital character. They deserve to be cherished *and lovingly restored where they have sometimes decayed. This sturdy no-nonsense front with the small window pane is typical of Western shops but the lettering is powerful and highly individualistic.*

Group of shops, Bailieborough, Co. Cavan
There are many fine old shop fronts in the wide main street of Bailieborough, but the group of Farrelly's shops is unique and delightful. The unifying factor here is the simple fluted Ionic column, a highly favoured motif which *appears all over the country. The rest of the design is very simple and unadorned with a single cornice over a common fascia. There are three different styles of lettering used. On the left the letters are attached porcelain, veined in imitation white marble. The central shop has cut-out wood letters,* *and the shop on the right has painted and simple shadowed letters. The spikes on the window sills are unsubtle and the message to loungers is clear. Restored and repainted this group of shops would be one of the most lively pieces of architecture in an already architecturally interesting town.*

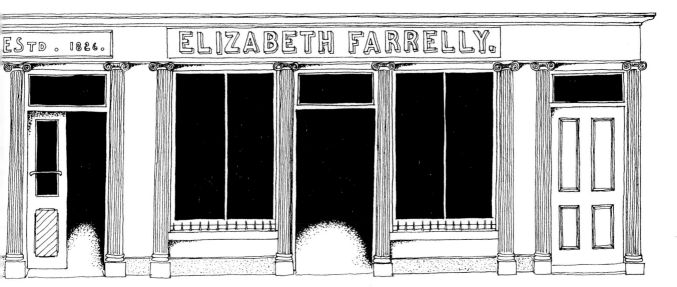

might explain why he had a series of specially designed ceramic tiles made for all of his shops. These had a motif of shamrocks intertwining with £s and were coloured green and cream. Lucinda Lambton in VANISHING VICTORIANA (1976) describes Thomas Lipton: *Sir Thomas was the first entrepreneur to introduce tea into the country as an everyday commodity rather than as a luxury item. With his slogan 'Direct from tea-garden to tea pot', he sold tea from his own plantations in Ceylon for one shilling a pound that was of the same quality as that which would fetch thirty-six guineas a pound at the Mincing Lane, London tea auctions! To advertise the first shipment's arrival in 1889, Sir Thomas (then Mr. Lipton – he was knighted by Queen Victoria in 1896) arranged for 200 men, bearing 80 tons of tea, to parade through Glasgow's streets in authentic Singhalese costume. His advertising was always extravagantly elaborate. 'Liptons Orphans' – pigs bought for the business and proclaimed by men with great banners – were paraded through the streets with Lipton painted on their backs. In 1881 a giant cheese, weighing three tons, was drawn around Glasgow by an elephant. . . . Thin men were made to carry banners 'Going to Liptons' while fat men carried banners 'Coming from Liptons'!*

Many of these multiple shops had branches in Ireland and along with the Irish multiple grocers the names of these stores were to be seen in cities and larger towns in their distinctive high quality name fascias and elaborate shop fronts – The Maypole Dairy Company, Findlaters, Leverett & Frye and Liptons.

House – Shop, Kilternan, Co. Dublin This house and shop includes a post office, a general grocery store and also sells hardware. It is thus a typical useful general store in a rural, farming and gardening area. The house is faced with local granite which is, strangely for a small house, in ashlar instead of the more practical and common random rubble. The neat name fascia has carved and decorated brackets and omits the more usual pilasters. The gutter of the house is supported on cut granite brackets which is a common Co. Dublin and Co. Wicklow detail and the verges have heavy barges to prevent the wind lifting the slates.

Pub–Grocer, Ranelagh, Dublin
The pub–grocer was a common combination in city and country until a few years ago. The link still occurs in country areas and closing time regulations stipulate screens and partitions nowadays, where in the past the screens were erected for privacy and separation. The men went to the bar while the women bought the groceries on the other side. In city areas only a limited grocery business is nowadays carried out in pubs and the 'grocer' sign on Humphreys is a relic of the past. This is one of the best preserved pub fronts left in the country. The building is in the splendid classical pilazzo style favoured by the publican families who lived in generously planned rooms over the shop and bar. This is a brick fronted building and whereas the facade was probably typical late Victorian red brick when completed, it is now lavishly oil painted in two tones and is a strikingly high quality building in the street. The pilasters have splendidly elaborate cappings and the lettering is raised and finely detailed and spaced. Note the toothed metal bars to prevent lounging on the window sills and the old mirror whiskey advertisement which acted as a screen in the window.

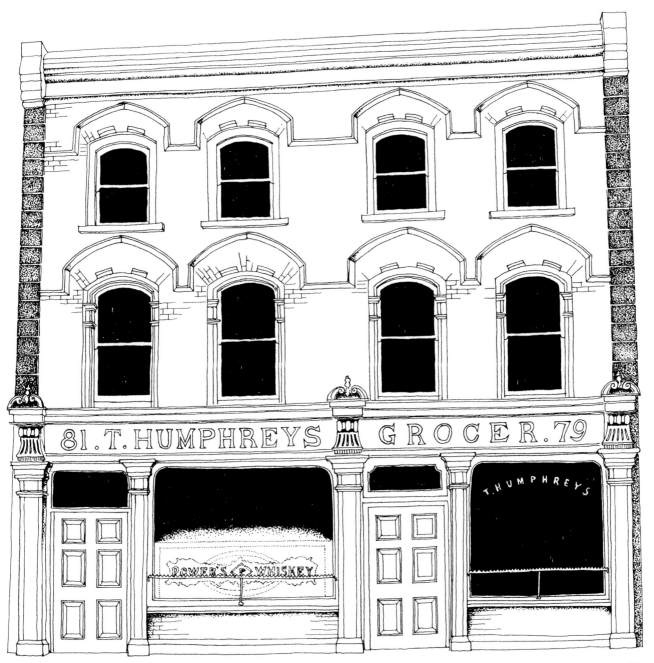

Grocer's Shop, Camden Street, Dublin
The family grocer in the city often lived over the shop and the larger enterprises produced an interesting and exclusive form for the combination of house and business. Cavey's of Camden Street, built in 1906, was a good solution to the problem on a rather narrow site. The narrowness is actually deliberately accentuated by the tall slim windows and the continuous shallow brick pilasters culminating in the pediment crowned with a finial. The living quarters are expressed by the Norman Shaw type oriel window and the composition is triumphantly finished at the top with balustrades and pediment with the date.

Grocery Shop, Sligo
In contrast to Minogue's shop, Bellew Brothers is a riot of detail demanding attention in a busy street. It is a fine example of the full-flowered late Victorian tradition of grocer's shop with rich embellishment of the front and a large plate glass display window. The fascia lettering is gold incised and matches the mirror advertisement with its gold painted letters.
The simple device of a classical pilaster with a cap holding up the bracket is abandoned in this case and the elaborately carved bracket merges with the pilaster to form an intricate and highly decorative framing for the shop front. A familiar feature of Victorian shop fronts was the sloping stall board in place of a sill. These were sometimes beautifully incised and made in polished brass or, as in this case, gold painted letters covered in plate glass. They acted both as advertisements and as deterrents to sitting down.

Shop, Mountshannon, Co. Clare
This shop typifies the tiny general
shop of a very small Irish village.
Mountshannon is beautifully situated
on the western shores of the huge
Lough Derg, the last great lake on the
River Shannon. The shop, in a terrace
of little houses in the tree-lined street, is
faced with large blocks of dressed
ashlar, while the plaster plinths are
painted bright red. The little dormer is
constructed in brick.
The simple name fascia is decorated
with wood dentils and painted red with
the letters picked out in white.

Grocer's Shop and Pub, Dunboyne,
Co. Meath
This shop is splendidly maintained and
is an excellent example of the high
quality wood shop fronts in country
districts. 'Grocer, Wines and Spirits'
was a commonly favoured description
of this type of business. The carved
wood brackets are particularly good on
these fronts.

Shop, Killaloe, Co. Clare
John Crotty's establishment is an
example of late nineteenth-century
expansionism in the general store
business. The grocery has now become
an 'Italian warehouse'. Architecturally
the grouping of the shop windows is
faultless. The problem of the steep
slope of the street is neatly resolved by
extending each bracket down to start
the new facia from the end of the
bracket. The stepped form of the
heavily modelled brackets and cornices
gives a most interesting and dynamic
effect to the narrow street. The brackets

are appropriately carved in forms of
fruit with large pineapples, bunches of
grapes and vines. The lettering is a
peculiarly Victorian invention, being
moulded in porcelain, veined to imitate
white marble. There are many
surviving examples of this form of
lettering throughout the country. The
different sizes of shop window and
different spacing of mullions did not
worry the designer, quite rightly, since
the strong articulation of the individual
shops with the carved pilasters and the
magnificent stepped fascia unified the
whole composition.

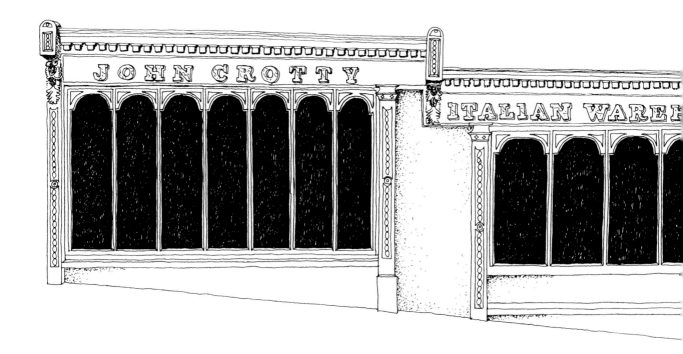

Shop, Graiguenamanagh, Co. Kilkenny

Joyce's general store is one of the best preserved shop fronts in this architecturally interesting town. The name fascia, carved gold painted letters covered by a plate glass fascia, is one of the finest in the country. The wood carved brackets and elaborate pilasters with colonettes are particularly fine and the large plate glass windows with the decorative corner pieces and thin mullions date this shop to the turn of the century. The front is a perfect, unspoiled example of the splendid type of provincial shop of the period.

Draper

Shop and House, Mitchelstown, Co. Cork

The two storey shop and house is probably the most common form for the family business in Ireland and is the next stage up from the modest single storey house with the shop in one of the front rooms. 'Noel's Fashion Salon' is a rather grandiose version of the type and is one of many excellent house and shop combinations in two or three storey versions along both sides of Mitchelstown's main street. Only a few of these shops have been destroyed at street level and a vigorous policy of restoration and conservation of the fronts would make this town an architectural gem.

Drapery shops on a large scale only became a feature of daily life in the later nineteenth century. In the country the people made their own clothes from home spun material while in the cities the rich had bespoke tailors. The tailors gradually developed shops to increase business but for the poor in the cities the cast off clothing of the rich was all that was available. Kellow Chesney in his detailed study THE VICTORIAN UNDERWORLD states that stealing clothes was the most frequently mentioned crime of the period. He said that secondhand woollen clothes were far superior to the damp-retaining cotton which was all the labouring class could afford: 'The musty odour of damp cotton fustian was held, like the smell of toasted herring, to be characteristic of the lower orders'. The alleys of the Victorian city were crowded with little open fronted shops each with masses of second hand clothes hanging outside.

The arrival of mass production with machines cutting out standard patterns reduced the price of clothes. Good suits and coats became available to all but very poor who had the street market for bargains.

*Draper's Shop, Newtownstewart, Co.
Tyrone*
The plate glass shop window was the
main design element of this shop of the
early twentieth century. The structural
columns are behind the glass. Note the
ventilators over the windows and the
large awnings concealed in a neat box
as part of the cornice. The gold and
glass lettering is particularly good.

*Draper's Shop and House,
Cahirciveen, Co. Kerry*
This house and shop is in the splendid
plaster tradition of Kerry. It is also a
good example of the traditional
solution to the design problem of
providing premises for a family
business. The living quarters are
strongly expressed in the pair of oriel
windows on the first floor – the top
floors being usually reserved for
bedrooms in this three storey version of
the plan.
The shop was a large and attractive
one for the period in this small town.
The diminutive balustrade with the
large date sign is architecturally
uncomfortable and illogical. However,
in townscape terms it is an endearing
conceit and along with the brash
elevational treatment forms a vital
element in the street.
The Irish language form for the
lettering 'The Irish House' was
probably inspired by the nationalism of
the period in the early 1920s although
the Celtic plaster decoration was part of
an earlier nineteenth-century tradition
common throughout the south.

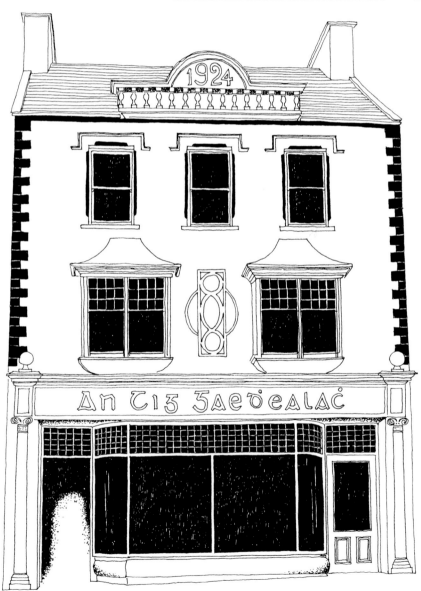

Boots and Shoes

Archaeological excavations around Christchurch Cathedral in Dublin found many traces of the craft industries of the early city. Boot and shoemaking was an active pursuit in the mediaeval city and this handcraft in leather persisted in Ireland with few changes almost into modern times. The first signs of mass production, as in all trades, probably began with the employment of several shoemakers to carry out different operations – the early assembly line. In 1846 Elias Howe invented the sewing machine and where previously the sole of the boot was fixed by tacks and hand stitched, the sewing machine speeded up production. In rural areas the craft of the shoemaker, unchanged for hundreds of years, very quickly declined in the late nineteenth century. New and improved shoe making machinery led quickly to mass produced footwear from large factories, which was of good quality and cheap. Pamela Horn stated that by 1890 a pair of machine made boots could be bought for about eight shillings, in contrast to the boots hand made by a rural craftsman costing about fourteen shillings.

The chain store shoe shops became a standard feature of even small towns from about 1900, and in the 1920s and 1930s were widespread and commanded practically all the sales of footwear. The village shoemaker became a shoe repairer and only a tiny minority of hand craftsmen remained to cater for more discerning customers.

Shoe Shop, Youghal, Co. Cork
The elaborately carved consoles of this shop are remarkable and although the shop front is late nineteenth or early twentieth century, there is still a classical elegance to the entablature.

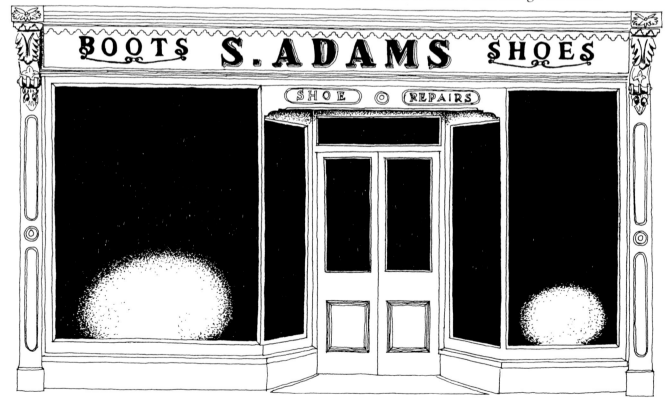

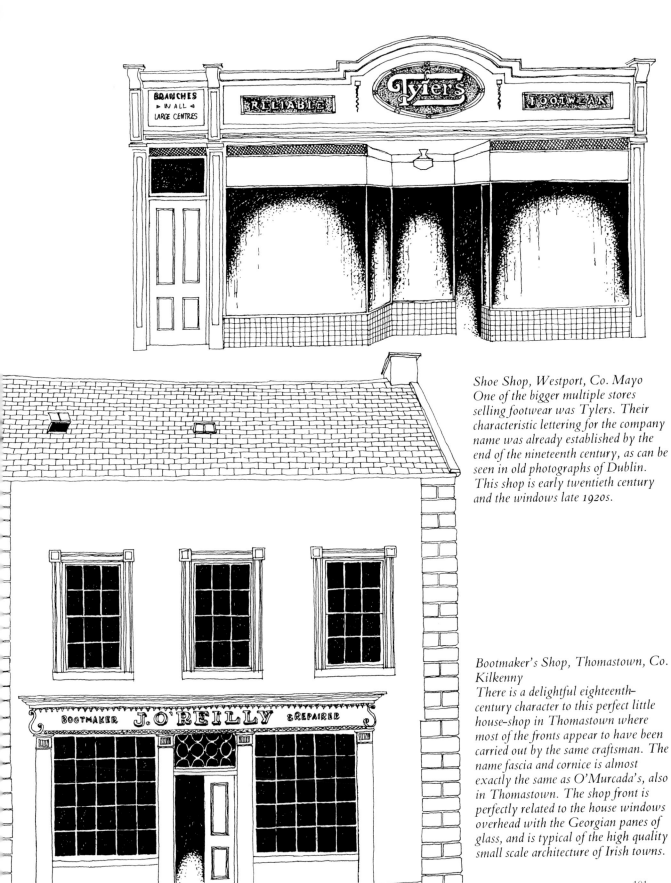

Shoe Shop, Westport, Co. Mayo
One of the bigger multiple stores selling footwear was Tylers. Their characteristic lettering for the company name was already established by the end of the nineteenth century, as can be seen in old photographs of Dublin. This shop is early twentieth century and the windows late 1920s.

Bootmaker's Shop, Thomastown, Co. Kilkenny
There is a delightful eighteenth-century character to this perfect little house-shop in Thomastown where most of the fronts appear to have been carried out by the same craftsman. The name fascia and cornice is almost exactly the same as O'Murcada's, also in Thomastown. The shop front is perfectly related to the house windows overhead with the Georgian panes of glass, and is typical of the high quality small scale architecture of Irish towns.

101

Jeweller, Watchmaker, Pawnbroker

The earliest jeweller's shops were attached to the workshops of the silversmiths and goldsmiths. There are numerous references in the CALENDAR OF ANCIENT RECORDS OF DUBLIN to goldsmiths and silversmiths being proposed as freemen of the city in the seventeenth century. The watchmaker is one of the few crafts to retain to this day the tradition of workplace combined with the shop.

Long after the practice of working in gold and silver on the premises gave way, in the nineteenth century, to larger sales of cheaper mass produced jewellery and watches, the tradition of keeping the names of the original crafts lived on. Richard's old shop in the Bull Ring in Wexford had carved gold painted italic script on the fascia announcing 'Goldsmith' and 'Silversmith'.

Some of the design features peculiar to jeweller's shops established themselves early on. Gerald Burke in TOWNSCAPES (1976) described an old shop in York: *Elegant eighteenth century bow shop front in Stonegate, York, with richly carved console brackets supporting carved fascia, fluted Corinthian columns, all painted black to set off silver and jewellery on display.* The tradition of black painted shop fronts, usually with gold leaf details, is almost exclusive to jewellers, watchmakers, antique shops, picture and print shops and in the past, to booksellers. In Ireland black is sometimes seen on chemists as in a magnificent Medical Hall in Navan, Co. Meath.

The tradition of richly carved wood detail on these shops is certainly strong in Ireland and many jeweller's shops, which were never very numerous in a sparsely populated country of not very wealthy people, are still manifcently preserved and suffer less than other shops from misguided 'improvements'.

The jewellers and watchmakers shops, in line with all other types in Ireland, kept their classical features despite exhortations from writers like Nathaniel Whittock who in his ILLUSTRATIONS OF THE SHOP FRONTS OF LONDON (1840) tried to sell the idea of Gothic for shop fronts: 'Goldsmiths, watch and clockmakers, book and print sellers, chemists and druggists might all use Gothic fronts with propriety'.

Victor Delassaux and John Elliott, architects, in their book of beautiful engravings of shop fronts STREET ARCHITECTURE, A SERIES OF SHOP FRONTS AND FACADES (1855) advised the use of Gothic lettering and that jeweller's shops should be '. . . dark chesnut or polished ebony with gilt mouldings'.

Jewellery Shop, Waterford City
Heine's shop is in characteristic black with the details picked out in red rather than in the traditional gold leaf. The lettering is whimsical, but the work of a highly self confident craftsman who was certainly original. The date of the shop is likely to be early twentieth century.

Clockmaker and Watchmaker, Fownes Street, Dublin
This perfect little shop is a surprising survivor in an area of the city which had massive rebuilding in the late nineteenth century. It is now dwarfed by the huge new Central Bank building and a glorious opportunity exists to preserve the bits of older Dublin around the piazza of the new building and keep a human scale at street level.

Pawnbrokers' shops existed from the middle ages and as Kellow Chesney states in THE VICTORIAN UNDERWORLD it was not only the poor who patronised the sign of the Three Balls. The middle classes and aristocracy pledged jewellery and plate, which establishes the link between pawnbrokers and jewellery shops, while the poor could only pledge clothes and bedding. However, pawnshops fulfilled a very important function in the nineteenth century. Dyos & Wolff in THE VICTORIAN CITY stated that 'the pawnshop was an urban institution ranking with the public house'. The new urban worker of the Industrial Revolution had a low income which made borrowing necessary when sickness interrupted his earnings, but the fact of having a reasonably regular income meant that his pledges could be redeeemed for future use. The pawnbroker, therefore, acted as the bank manager does today, to help maintain a balance.

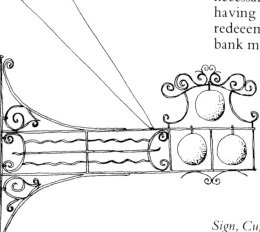

Sign, Cuffe Street, Dublin
The three brass balls are traditionally the trade sign of the pawnbroker and the sign is reputed to have originally denoted the premises of a Lombard merchant. This sign is a more elaborate version of the usual simple one and is a beautiful addition to an old street which is being gradually wiped out in favour of the motor car.

Pawnbroker's Shop, Cuffe Street, Dublin
The sign on Gorman's, 'Loans on every description of valuable property', appears to be a traditional form which has survived. A political cartoon in PUNCH *of 1851 shows the doorway of a pawnshop with the sign 'Money Lent upon every Description of Valuable Property'.*

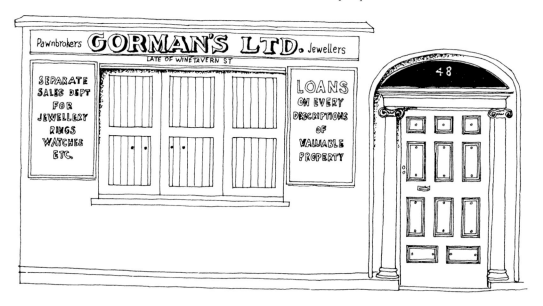

Watchmaker and Jeweller's Shop,
Birr, Co. Offaly
This superb shop is a perfect example
of the rich enclosures which the
jewellers decided were necessary to set
off their seductive wares. For such a
small shop the wood carving detail is
astonishing, from the egg and dart
moulded cornice to the large and
assured cappings of the pilasters. The
lettering is one of the best examples in
the country of the highly decorative
three tone, top shadowed style. The
strong and sturdy wood shutters are
beautifully crafted and detailed and
they are not allowed to spoil the
appearance of the shop front when
closed. This is a lesson which could be
learned by the modern metal shutter
manufacturers who have been allowed
to turn centre city streets into monstrous
dead canyons at night and at week-
ends.

Pawnbroker's Shop, Clanbrassil Street
Lower, Dublin
Kilbride's splendidly robust
Corinthian pilasters are painted in the
traditional black. The lettering is out of

character with the shop design and is
almost certainly of 1930s vintage, but
for all that it is strong and simple and a
lively addition to an old street which is
being abandoned and run down.

Hardware, Ironmonger

The ironmonger's, which later became the hardware shop, was one of the most important stores for nineteenth-century country people. Photographs from the Lawrence collection of Irish small town streets show clearly the wealth of hardware goods stocked by these shops and we can guess the conditions of life which necessitated the goods on display. A photograph of South Main Street, Wexford about 1900 shows 'Sinnott & Sons' lettered in mock marble with an old projecting sign overhead consisting of a large ancient key and 'Ironmongery Warehouse'. Hanging outside the window are bundles of brushes – large coarse brushes for yard sweeping and large and small whitewash brushes for farmhouse and wall painting. Coils of wire in the doorway, and kettles, ladles and crockery made up the window display. Another photograph of the Main Street shows a shop which announces itself as the agent for a Dye Works and as the 'Cheapest House for wallpaper, window glass, paints, oils, varnishes, etc.'. This shop has house brooms, feather dusters, baskets and pictures, hanging from the frames.

In earlier times the metal tools and objects required by country people were made by the local smith. Estyn Evans in IRISH FOLK WAYS gives details of the modest iron candle and light holders and other domestic items which the country people used. The most important item of ironmongery was the spade. This was made by the local blacksmith until the water driven tilt hammer made mass production possible and the hardware shop replaced the smith for sales of tools.

Hardware shop fronts did not develop any characteristics peculiar to the trade. The wide nature of the variety of the goods stocked, however, led to a bazaar type appearance with masses of implements and objects stacked and hung outside and spilling on to the pavement.

Victor Delasseux and John Elliott in STREET ARCHITECTURE suggested different styles for the shop fronts of the various trades. The ironmonger and brazier was advised to create a Gothic iron facade: 'A little extra expense in the facade will not be thrown away in this business, the front affording the best opportunity of shewing what the proprietor can effect with the material in which he deals.' Their engraving of an ironmonger's shop was a delightful fantasy in cast iron, with almost a wall of plate glass broken by slim double mullions with glazed inserts.

Nineteenth-century photographs of cities and towns show the remarkable wealth of the ironworkers' craft in the many beautiful hang brackets, some carrying lights and signs, all along the streets. It is sometimes possible to spot a few remnants of these, without their lamps or lettering, remaining above the level of the shop fronts in many towns.

Hardware Shop, Youghal, Co. Cork
The cast iron frill with end finials would certainly appear to advertise the ironmonger's craft, but these decorations were commonplace on all types of shops in the nineteenth-century street. The shop windows were designed for large sheets of plate glass but the scale was still held by the central division and the graceful curve to the top of the glass. The lettering is modern and is an excellent example of the live craft of one of the signwriters who still works in the area.

Hardware Shop, Tullow, Co. Carlow
Splendidly painted red and yellow, this shop is an excellent example of fairly primitive but intuitively good design which was a feature of so many simple shop fronts of country towns. The columns with their strange round caps projecting up into the fascia are *unusual, but a very attractive feature. The cornice, fretted with its simple strong dentils, is exactly functional. It protects and emphasises the name fascia, a trick which seems to have been forgotten on many modern designs. The windows were almost certainly divided into smaller panes in the past.*

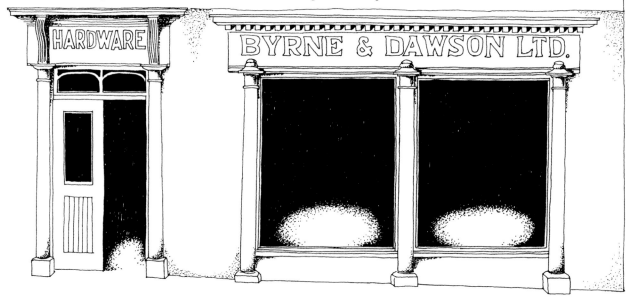

A nineteenth-century hardware shop in Athy, Co. Kildare

Bookmaker

Bookmaker's Shop, Westport, Co. Mayo
In small country towns the bookmaker' shop was often tiny – a characteristic also of the country solicitor and auctioneer.

In the eighteenth century and well into the early part of the nineteenth century, bookmaking was hardly a profession, although gambling was a widespread occupation. Betting was conducted at private clubs and was in the nature of 'gentleman to gentleman' transactions. In the middle of the nineteenth century in Britain, horse racing became popular and the masses of lower middle class and labourers contributed their small bets to make a huge total for the bookmaker. Kellow Chesney in THE VICTORIAN UNDERWORLD graphically describes the rise of the urban betting shop which often started in a tobacconists. However, he states that: 'in the eyes of authority they were a scandalous nuisance, actively encouraging disorder and lack of thrift among the lower classes'. In 1853 the law was used to close betting shops but, of course, gambling went on and formed a new underworld.

A cartoon in PUNCH in 1852 was entitled 'Bolted!' and showed a scene outside a betting office with a disconsolate looking crowd, in tall hats, after the bookmaker has absconded with their winnings.

In Ireland, bookmakers, grandly called 'Turf Accountants', do not make the interiors too comfortable or attractive, in line no doubt with the Victorian disapproval of idleness.

Bookmaker's Shop, Dungarvan, Co. Waterford
Bookmakers' shops were usually unobtrusive but the ebullient good taste and love of craft of the Irish shop fitter did not allow regulations or traditions to prevent him from producing a lively design. In Corcoran's the window is partly obscured with black paint to prevent scandal and observation from the street, but the curved letters in white liven the dead surface. The columns with their little turned caps are in the best tradition of Irish street architecture.

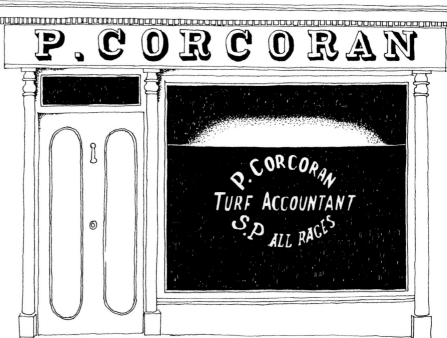

The Small Shop

Old Shop, Coalisland, Co. Tyrone

HIGH CLASS CONFECTIONERY

O'REILLY'S

Old Shop, Collooney, Co. Sligo

House and Shop, Cork city

Pub-Shop, Annascaul, Co. Kerry
This very old building on the Dingle peninsula demonstrates an early example of plaster work following directly in the older stone tradition. The feature over the door is in the tradition of the stone hood mouldings of castles and churches but the little plaster motifs are again typical of similar features found in Co. Kerry. The plaster bands which link the shoulders of the hood with the plinth are simple and decorous.

115

Glossary of Architectural Terms

Ashlar:	Squared blocks of cut stone laid in regular courses
Astragal:	A small moulding of circular section
Balustrade:	Series of short posts supporting a rail
Barge:	Finish to gable ends of roofs
Bracket:	A projection used as a support
Capital:	The top of a column or pilaster
Casement window:	A window hinged at one side to open in or out
Chamfer:	A cut-away square angle forming an oblique surface
Collonnade:	A row of columns supporting an entablature
Colonette:	A little column
Column:	A vertical supporting post
Console:	A bracket in the form of a scroll
Corinthian column:	One of the classical orders. The capital is usually ornamented with acanthus or other leaves
Cornice:	A moulded projection crowning a wall, window or entablature
Cyma recta:	A double curved moulding, upper part concave, lower convex
Dentil:	Small rectangular blocks like a row of teeth, under a cornice
Diamond pointed rustication:	Masonry cut in blocks with deep joints, each stone cut in the form of low pyramids
Doorcase:	Framing, in plaster or stone, around a door
Doorpost:	Vertical members supporting the door frames

Doric column:	One of the classical orders. The capital has simple mouldings
Dutch gable:	A curved gable
Egg and dart:	Alternating pointed and oval motifs usually in an ovolo moulding
Engaged column:	A column attached to a wall
Entablature:	The upper part of an order consisting of cornice, frieze and architrave
Fascia:	A flat band, usually the name board, over a shop window
Festoon:	A garland of flowers, fruit or leaves suspended in a curve
Fillet:	A narrow flat band used to separate two mouldings or two surfaces
Finial:	An ornament used to crown a pediment, gable roof or spire
Flutes:	Vertical grooves, usually curved, in a column or pilaster
Foliated:	A surface with leaf ornaments
Frieze:	The part of an entablature between the cornice and the architrave or a decorative band
Frill:	A decorative railing or lacy band
Functionalism:	The creed of fitness for purpose being the primary consideration
Hood moulding:	A projection to throw off rainwater, usually over windows or doors
Ionic column:	One of the classical orders. The capital is formed of volutes
Modillion:	One of a series of blocks or brackets usually under a cornice
Mullion:	A vertical dividing member of a window

Nailhead:	An ornament shaped like a little pyramid
Nameboard:	The fascia of a shop front
Obelisk:	A four sided tapering shaft with a pyramidal top
Oriel window:	A bay window or projecting window, usually from an upper storey
Ovolo:	A convex shaped moulding
Parapet:	A low wall usually above the cornice of a building
Pedestal:	A support at the base of a column or statue
Pediment:	A triangular gable usually over an entablature or over doors and windows as an ornamental feature
Pilaster:	A rectangular column projecting slightly from a wall
Plinth:	A projecting base to a wall
Quoin:	The external angle to a building and the rusticated stones or treatment of the corner
Random rubble:	Walls built of rough uncut stones
Rosette:	A circular ornament in the form of a rose
Sash window:	Double hung vertical sliding window
Scotia:	A small concave moulding
Soffit:	The undersurface of a feature
Spandril:	The triangular area between two adjacent arches or to the side of one arch
Stall board:	Boards, usually sloping, on shop window sills, usually with names
Storey post:	Vertical posts of a timber framed wall
String course:	A projecting moulding or band running horizontally across a facade
Stucco:	Plasterwork
Transom:	A horizontal dividing member in a window
Trefoil:	Three small arc openings, usually in shop window spandrils
Tuscan column:	One of the classical orders. A simplified Doric
Volute:	A scroll in the form of a spiral. The distinctive feature of an Ionic capital
Weathering:	The inclined top of a projection to throw off water

Select Bibliography

Adburgham, Alison, SHOPS AND SHOPPING 1800–1914, London 1964.

Amery, Colin, 3 CENTURIES OF ARCHITECTURAL CRAFTSMANSHIP, London 1977.

Barnard, Julian, *Some work by W. J. Neatby*, THE CONNOISSEUR (Nov. 1970).

Barnard, Julian, *The Master of Harrod's Meat Hall*, APOLLO (March 1970).

Barnard, Julian *W. J. Neatby and Ceramic Tiles*. THE ARCHITECT (Sept. 1971).

Betjeman, John, ENGLISH CITIES AND SMALL TOWNS, London 1943.

Braddell, D'Arcy, *Little Shops of Paris*, ARCHITECTURAL REVIEW (July 1926).

Briggs, Asa, VICTORIAN CITIES, London 1975.

Burke, Gerald, TOWNSCAPES, London 1976.

Chesney, Kellow, THE VICTORIAN UNDERWORLD, London 1970.

Crook, J. Mordaunt, VICTORIAN ARCHITECTURE, A VISUAL ANTHOLOGY, New York: London 1971.

Cullen, Gordon, THE CONCISE TOWNSCAPE, London 1961.

Cullen, L. M., LIFE IN IRELAND, London 1968.

Curl, James Stephens, VICTORIAN ARCHITECTURE, London 1973.

Dan and Willmott, ENGLISH SHOP FRONTS OLD & NEW, London 1907.

Davis, Dorothy, A HISTORY OF SHOPPING, London 1966.

Dean, David, ENGLISH SHOP FRONTS FROM CONTEMPORARY SOURCE BOOKS 1792–1840, London 1970.

Delasseux, Victor and Elliott, John, STREET ARCHITECTURE, 1855.

Dixon, Hugh, ULSTER ARCHITECTURE, Ulster Architectural Heritage Society, 1976.

Ireland

Shops illustrated or places mentioned

N

Coleraine
DERRY
Dungiven
Ballymena
Convoy
Strabane
Magherafelt
Newtownstewart
Stewartstown
Omagh
Coalisland
BELFAST
Dungannon
Donegal

Grange
Sligo
Collooney

Bailieborough
Carrickmacross
Mullagh
Kingscourt
Ardee
Castlebar
Kells
Westport
Castlepollard
Navan
Louisburg
Delvin
Rathmolyon
Summerhill
Dunboyne
DUBLIN
GALWAY
Kilternan
Bray

Portumna
Birr
Athy
Mountshannon
Ennistymon
Tullow
Ennis
Killaloe
Kilkenny
Muinebeag
Bunclody
LIMERICK
Thomastown
Askeaton
Graiguenamanagh
Enniscorthy
Newcastlewest
Ballyduff
Bruff
Listowel
Carrick-on-suir
Wexford
Abbeyfeale
Mitchelstown
Waterford
Anascaul
Castleisland
Kildorrery
Dingle
Mallow
Dungarvan
Killorglin
Cahirciveen
CORK
Youghal

Skibbereen

0 10 20 30 40 50 MILES

80 KMS

125

Cake Shop, Mullagh, Co. Cavan